Violence Against Women

A Critique of the Sociobiology of Rape

Edited by
Suzanne R. Sunday and Ethel Tobach

A GENES AND GENDER MONOGRAPH

GENES AND GENDER SERIES

Ethel Tobach and Betty Rosoff, Editors

GORDIAN PRESS
NEW YORK 1985

First published 1985 by Gordian Press

Library of Congress Cataloging in Publication Data
Main entry under title:

Violence against women.

    (A Genes and gender monograph)
    Includes index.
    1. Rape — Addresses, essays, lectures.   2. Sociobiology — Addresses,
essays, lectures.   3. Violence — Research — Addresses, essays, lectures.
I. Sunday, Suzanne R.   II. Tobach, Ethel, 1921–   III. Series.
HV6558.V56   1985   362.8'83   85–14729
ISBN 0-87752-231-6

CONTENTS

PREFACE

As editors of the Genes and Gender Series, we are proud to present this monograph, the first in a series exposing the application of genetic determinism to justify racist and sexist theories and activities. Continuing our policy of reporting the current status of this problem in the scientific community, this volume offers information on the topic of rape derived from research; discussions of the implications of the way the research is formulated; and the significance of the results of this research for society. Above all, the articles in this book make it possible for the reader to evaluate the popularly written, visually seductive and pseudo-authoritative material in the various forms of media which consistently advertise a hereditarian view.

ETHEL TOBACH AND BETTY ROSOFF

ACKNOWLEDGEMENTS

We wish to thank the following people who have helped us produce this book: Florence Brauner, Pat Brunauer, Kenneth Kurzweil, Ruth Newman, and Ronnie Tuft. Additionally, we wish to thank those who shared with us their material and experiences: Lila Braine, Irene Frieze, David Miller, Allan Mirsky, Marlene Oscar Berman, Rhoda Unger, and Martha Wilson. Finally, we wish to thank Marge Piercy for giving us permission to reprint a portion of her poem, "Rape Poem."

Rape Poem

There is no difference between being raped
and being pushed down a flight of cement steps
except that the wounds also bleed inside.

There is no difference between being raped
and being run over by a truck
except that afterward men ask if you enjoyed it.

There is no difference between being raped
and being bit on the ankle by a rattlesnake
except that people ask if your skirt was short
and why you were out alone anyhow.

There is no difference between being raped
and going head first through a windshield
except that afterward you are afraid
not of cars
but half the human race.

— MARGE PIERCY*

*Excerpted from "Rape Poem" by Marge Piercy, 1976, In *Living in the open*. New York: Knopf. Copyright by Marge Piercy. Reprinted by permission of Marge Piercy.

PROLOGUE

The genesis of this book exemplifies an auspicious development in the scientific community; scientific theories are no longer under the scrutiny of specialists only. Under the influence of the equal rights movements, populations of various disenfranchised and unrepresented individuals have begun to *make* scientific history, not only to study it. They are the investigators, and not merely the subjects of the investigations. The events which led to the publication of these papers illustrate this process.

The appearance of articles by W. D. Hamilton (e.g., 1964) offering a solution to an apparent paradox in Darwinian evolutionary theory received relatively little notice by those who were not evolutionary biologists, ecologists, or members of related disciplines. E. O. Wilson's publication (1975), on the other hand, was differently received. It was widely read and discussed outside of the traditional disciplines concerned with the evolution of social behavior. Not only were the tenets of this ideology presented in all media, but they were eagerly examined and frequently adopted as pertinent to many fields of biology and by many in the humanities, medicine, and the social sciences. As indicated in the articles in the present book, genetic determinism is the basic concept of sociobiology; it is therefore not surprising that every aspect of human behavior became the target for reanalysis in the light of sociobiological precepts. Among these was the subject of rape.

In 1980, R. Thornhill published a report of his research with scorpionflies and made a generalization about the similarity of forced copulation in animals and human rape. From this analogy he continued by pointing out shared reproductive strategies of humans and other animals. It was in this article that he proposed "a general rape hypothesis."

The response to this article was mostly within the scientific community; however, as the following demonstrates, other responses were developing. The precipitating event leading to the publication of this book stems from the traditions of part of the psychological community. It is the custom of the Division for Comparative and Physiological Psychology of the American Psychological Association (Division 6, APA) to invite newly elected fellows to that Division to give a "Fellow's Address" at the annual convention of the APA. Accordingly, Delbert D. Thiessen of the University of Texas, accepted the invitation tendered him by David Miller of the University of Connecticut, who was the chair of the Program Committee for the Division that year (1983). The title of Dr. Thiessen's talk was "Rape as a Reproductive Strategy: Our Evolutionary Legacy." This was duly received, and printed in the preliminary program mailed to members of the Division before the Convention took place in August of that year.

In July 1983, Lila Ghent Braine, of Barnard College and a fellow of Division 6, sent a letter to Dr. Miller in which she called the title of Thiessen's paper, "offensive to women" and, she hoped, to many men as well. She sent a copy of that letter (see Appendix A) to the then President of Division 6, Allan F. Mirsky, of the National Institute of Mental Health, and to Dr. Thiessen. Neither of them replied to her letter. She did receive an answer from Dr. Miller, who agreed that the title was "provocative" but concluded, "As Program Chair, I am very eager to give him that opportunity rather than to, in any way, attempt to censure his viewpoints." (See Appendix B).

On August 4, 1983, Martha Wilson, also a Fellow of Division 6 and a faculty member of the University of Connecticut (where David Miller is also a faculty member), wrote Miller (Appendix C) that she found Thiessen's title offensive, tasteless, and senseless. She called for promotion of, "an awareness of APA's scientific virtues, rather than the image of Psychology that we are all too familiar with in the popular press," as well as the creation of a climate such that, "the possibility of confusing or offending could be minimized." David Miller gave Dr. Wilson a response similar to that given Dr. Braine (Appendix D). Neither Dr. Mirsky nor Dr. Thiessen (both of whom had received copies of Dr. Wilson's letter) answered her.

The Secretary-Treasurer of the Division, Marlene Oscar Berman, who chaired the session at the Convention (August 1983) at which Dr. Thiessen spoke reported that "there was a heated discussion after the talk, but Thiessen was unwilling to continue it in another room, despite the fact that a room had been arranged for such discourse." (See Appendix E.)

Following his talk, Loraine Obler, a neuropsychologist with the Veterans Administration, wrote a statement for the Association for

Women in Psychology (AWP) which was read at the Open Forum of the Convention, a platform through which members of the Association can present their views on matters of interest to psychologists (see Appendix F). Their statement says that "while we have serious doubts about the intellectual underpinnings of Thiessen's work on rape, . . . we support his right to report his ideas. What we find *in*-supportable is the provocative and inflammatory, sensational way he chooses to publicize himself at the expense of women." According to the statement, Dr. Thiessen had not responded to their several attempts to discuss his paper before the conference.

In October 1983, Irene Hanson Frieze of the University of Pittsburgh, and the then President of the Division of the Psychology of Women (Division 35, APA), speaking for the Executive Committee of that Division, expressed their view in a letter to Dr. Thiessen. They found, "the implicit acceptance of the idea of rape as a reasonable means of having children quite upsetting." They were also surprised to hear him defend the title after his talk (see Appendix G). In Dr. Thiessen's answer to Dr. Frieze, he states that his aim:

> . . . in part, is similar to that of most women, namely to be able to reduce the incidence of rape. . . . Is my assumption correct that you do want to understand the facts of rape in order to do something constructive about it? . . . Perhaps you believe that a biological approach assumes genetic determinism, and hence suggests that behaviors are unmodifiable. That is certainly not the case. All behaviors, particularly those of evolutionarily complex species, depend upon interactions between genes and environment. Rape, therefore, may have a phylogenetic heritage, in that it appears to be associated with a polygynous mating style, but is also facultative, changing dramatically with socioeconomic, sociological and psychological conditions. (See Appendix H.)

As there is no published statement by Dr. Thiessen about his views on how his sociobiological approach, derived from genetic determinism, leads to the modification of the behavior of rapists through some process involving socioeconomic, sociological and psychological conditions (see Tobach and Sunday, Epilogue), it is difficult to assess his objections to the statement by Division 35. As of this writing, so far as we know, no copies of the talk given by Dr. Thiessen have been made available.

Two articles were published in *Ethology and Sociobiology* at the end of 1983. These articles contended that taking an evolutionary (sociobiological) perspective would increase our understanding of human rape. William and Lea Shields and Randy and Nancy Wilmsen Thornhill, in their articles entitled respectively, Forcible Rape: An Evolutionary Perspective, and Human Rape: An Evolutionary Analysis; proposed that rape among humans was a reproductive strategy which had provided the rapists with increased reproductive success. Thus, rape was a behavior pattern which had been selected for.

The issues raised in these articles and in the exchanges about Thiessen's talk called for a serious discussion of the sociobiologists' premises with regard to rape. Accordingly, a symposium at the meeting of the Eastern Psychological Association in spring of 1984 was organized by Ethel Tobach and chaired by Suzanne Sunday. The session was well attended and there were many requests for copies of the papers read. In response, the Genes and Gender Collective decided to publish expanded versions of these papers as the first of a monograph series.

During the preparation of the manuscripts for publication, it was clear that another dimension was desirable. Accordingly, Julia and Herman Schwendinger, whose excellent book on the subject of rape was just published, were invited to write a chapter which would add the sociological/anthropological approach.

Some words on formulations which underlay the editing of this book are in order. It is understandable that in writing on a topic as circumscribed as the sociobiology of rape, there would be some overlap in the material. It was decided to leave the relatively small amount of redundancy in the volume because each writer presents slightly different emphases and insight to the citations. There is, as one would expect, some difference of opinion and interpretation.

Because women and other minorities have come to understand the interconnectedness of consciousness and language, we believe it was useful for us to impress our views in regard to the language to be used, by editing the papers as follows.

It was decided that when talking of women and men, the terms "female" and "male" would not be used, except as adjectives when the writer(s) felt more comfortable using those terms rather than "feminine" and "masculine." However, if reference was being made to the gamete-producing characteristics of all species, including the human species, the terms "male" and "female" were considered appropriate. When particular terms had historical or societal meaning that should not be lost, as in "male chauvinism," "male supremacy" or "race," the words were put in quotes to indicate their historical perspective.

In the same way, we chose to make a distinction between the words "sex" and "gender." When issues of human equality and societal position are involved, the appropriate word, we believe, is "gender." When the issue of reproductive function or reproductive behavior is of concern, the word "sex" or "sexual" is more germane.

We view this volume as a commencement not only of the Genes and Gender monograph series, but as a contribution to the formulation of the serious research which must be carried out to understand why men violently abuse women. It is also hoped that we will have stimulated behavioral and biological researchers to reexamine the assumptions underlying their research and the significance of the language they use to discuss their conclusions. It is only by understanding the processes which lead to the catastrophic behavior of human rape that some hopefully constructive course of action can be carried out to prevent its occurrence in the future.

ETHEL TOBACH

SUZANNE R. SUNDAY

MARCH 1985

REFERENCES

Hamilton, W. D. (1964). The genetic theory of social behavior, I, II. *Journal of Theoretical Biology, 7,* 1–52.

Shields, W. M. & Shields, L. M. (1983). Forcible rape: An evolutionary perspective. *Ethology and Sociobiology, 4,* 115–136.

Thornhill, R. (1980). Rape in *Panorpa* scorpionflies and a general rape hypothesis. *Animal Behaviour, 28,* 52–59.

Thornhill, R. & Thornhill, N. W. (1983). Human rape: An evolutionary analysis. *Ethology and Sociobiology, 4,* 137–173.

Wilson, E. O. (1975). *Sociobiology: The new synthesis.* Cambridge, MA: The Belknap Press of Harvard University Press.

INTRODUCTION

Suzanne R. Sunday
MANHATTANVILLE COLLEGE

There has been an ongoing debate concerning sociobiology and the genetic basis of human behavior since Wilson's 1975 publication (e.g. Bleier, 1984; Caplan, 1978; Lewontin, Rose, and Kamin, 1984; Montagu, 1980; Rosoff and Tobach, 1978–1985; Sahlins, 1976). In late 1983 two papers, Shields and Shields, and Thornhill and Thornhill, appeared which formally applied the sociobiological theory to forced sexual behavior in humans — rape. Although the idea that rape could confer some type of adaptive advantage to the rapist had been previously suggested for non-human species, this was the first time such an idea had been systematically applied to humans and supposedly substantiated by data.

It is the purpose of this book to critically examine the applicability of a sociobiological interpretation of rape both in humans and in other animals. This introductory chapter provides an overview of the work which has suggested that rape is adaptive and examines the various definitions of rape that have been used and some of the implications of the view that rape has an evolutionary root. Lenington's chapter focuses on the theory of sociobiology. It provides a discussion of the roots of sociobiology and the theoretical assumptions of human sociobiology and finally extends to the work on rape. In chapter three, Harding critically examines the animal data which have been used to support the hypothesis of the sociobiology of rape. The social psychology of rape is explored in the chapter written by Denmark and Friedman. They review the myths concerning human rape and the implications of such myths for both victims and society as a whole. They end with a description of the incidence of rape in the United States. The Schwendingers' chapter provides a discussion of the cross-cultural data concerning rape. The effects of the language used in addressing the issue of rape are explored by Blackman. She addresses this on a societal level and the level of the rape victim. The final chapter, written by Tobach and Sunday, deals with the social psychology of the response of the psychological community to studies of rape. A theoretical formulation is offered to replace genetic determinist and interactionist explanations of behavior.

THE ADAPTIVE NATURE OF RAPE

Charles Darwin (1871) was the first to suggest that males and females of a given species could have evolved under differing selection pressures. This concept of sexual selection has been applied to both physical and behavioral traits since that time. Although Darwin did discuss differences between the sexes and the evolutionary basis of these differences, he did not mention rape.

One of the first scientists to suggest explicitly that rape had been selected for in humans was Freud's student, Helene Deutsch (1944). She believed that sexual behavior in hominids was profoundly changed when females became sexually receptive at all times rather than having only a short period of receptivity (estrus) as do most mammals. She felt that estrus periods, which were usually signaled visually and/or olfactorily, left sexual activity under female control. When hominids lost estrus, Deutsch felt that the female had "subordinated herself to the sexual will and domination of the male." (p.227) She continued further by saying, "With the displacement of the body's center of gravity, the development of the upright posture, and the formation of powerful prehensile appendages, the male could free himself from his dependence upon the feminine rhythm and take sexual possession of the female even without her consent" (p.228). Although Deutsch related this to her ideas of female masochism, she clearly felt that men had evolved to be rapists.

From 1930 to 1970, the term rape was used in the ethology literature to describe field observations of highly aggressive mating attempts by males toward resisting females. Rape was reported in a variety of species of ducks and geese (e.g. Lorenz, 1970, 1971; Smith, 1968), lizards, and rooks (see Lorenz, 1970 for a review of these findings). Tinbergen (1965) also reported a connection between sexual behavior and attack behavior in gulls and guppies. Rape-like behaviors were reported in non-natural settings. Meyer-Holzapfel (1968) for example, reported hypersexual and aggressive responses in male zoo animals towards non-estrus females. Calhoun (1962) found that some male Norway rats living in a severely overcrowded enclosure mounted and attacked non-estrus, unwilling females.

During the 1970s and 1980s, rape was reported as occurring in a variety of animal species in their natural environment (see Harding's chapter in this volume for more information). The appearance of "naturally occurring" rape prompted many researchers to suggest that males who raped gained some type of advantage. Parker (1974) stated that attempted rape may allow a male to gain fitness (increase the likelihood of reproducing) if the resulting hybrid's fitness is sufficiently high, if the time investment necessary for the male to rape is not too great, if the female can be overpowered, and if the sperm can compete to fertilize the egg. Unfortunately, none of the research on rape in animals has provided any evidence indicating that the fitness of the rapist actually increased due to his having raped.

Many sociobiologists took these reports of rape and generalized to humans. For example, Thornhill and Thornhill (1983) state, "The rapist behaves as if he is sexually motivated; indeed as if he is trying to reproduce." (p. 163). Barash (1979) says, "Perhaps human rapists, in their own criminally misguided way, are doing the best they can to maximize their fitness." (p. 55). Wartime raping was reported as, "having made good reproductive sense during our long warrior history" (MacKinnon, 1978, p. 226). He did, however, emphasize that not all forms of rape are adaptive. Symons (1979), although not explicitly supporting the idea that rape is an adaptation in the human male, does emphasize that males prefer impersonal sexual interactions involving little or no cost; rape can indeed be considered such a sexual encounter. Reminiscent of Deutsch's theory, Alexander and Noonan (1979) stated that when estrus was lost and concealed ovulation appeared in hominid females, males no longer knew when the females were ovulating. They suggested that rape might be a feasible strategy for achieving some reproduction under these circumstances.

Thornhill (1980) also felt that rape had an evolutionary root. He, like Deutsch, said that, "larger males were favoured because of the increased likelihood of successful rape" (p. 57). In the 1980 paper, and again in Thornhill and Thornhill's 1983 paper, it was stated that rape is a strategy primarily employed by men who did not have access to adequate resources and could not, therefore, attract a female in more conventional ways. Without raping, these men might not reproduce. Further, it suggests that rape should be found only in species where females depend upon the resources provided by the male to be able to reproduce. Although the articles claim that these are testable hypotheses, no data are provided to indicate that rape increases a male's reproductive success or that male resources are necessary for reproduction.

Shields and Shields (1983) also view rape as one reproductive strategy of the human male. They distinguish three types of mating strategies: honest courtship, deceitful or manipulative courtship and rape. In honest courtship, a male does intend to provide his resources and his time to the female and their resulting offspring. Deceitful courtship occurs when a male offers to provide paternal investment so that he might copulate with a given female. Following copulation, however, he deserts her. If a male is unable to mate in either of these two ways, he could still reproduce by raping. "We suspect that during human evolutionary history, males that possessed a mating strategy that included rape as a facultative response were favored by natural selection over those that did not" (p. 123). According to the Shields', the proximate cause of human rape may be anger or hostility, but the ultimate cause is enhancement of male fitness.

Although they do discuss rape as an adaptive strategy, they do not imply that all males rape nor do they imply that men who rape do not show honest courtship or deceitful courtship in other circumstances. They state that the mating strategy adopted by a given man will depend upon an unconscious analysis of both the costs (time, energy, etc.) and the benefits (an increase in fitness) of such behavior. They present data which they feel substantiate their theory. They do not, however, provide any data which demonstrates an increase in a man's fitness resulting from his raping behavior. Data showing a significant number of viable pregnancies resulting from rape would have to be presented in order to support their conclusions.

THE DEFINITION OF RAPE

A major problem throughout the literature concerning animal and human rape has been an inconsistency in the working definitions of the term, "rape." For most people, the definition of rape in humans seems very straightforward. Rape is generally defined as sexual behavior without consent. This definition is not, however, the same one which as been used historically, judicially, or in empirical or theoretical examinations of rape.

Brownmiller (1975) summarized previous societal definitions of rape and found many to focus on the theft of virginity (thus necessitating vaginal penetration by a penis) without appropriate payment to the woman's family. This often meant that the proper price or a marriage proposal could lead to the dropping of the charge of rape. It also distinguished between the rape of an unmarried woman and the rape of a married woman, with the former being a far more serious offense. Even today, most states disallow the use of the word rape if a wife is accusing her husband of sex against her will.

The use of the term rape in animal research presents further problems. Often researchers anthropomorphize and assume that nonhuman behaviors which look like rape, are rape. Additionally, rape is often implied rather than operationally defined. An examination of animal studies in which the term rape is used reveals a wide range of definitions.

Animal rape almost always is defined as copulation forced on a female by a male. (The one exception to this is the study by Abele and Gilchrist, 1977, where they labeled the "cementing" of the genitals of one male worm by another male worm as rape because the "rapist" is more likely to pass on his genes due to the lack of competition by the "raped" worm). The use of the term forced with respect to rape is problematic. Some definitions of rape require aggressive behavior by the male and overt resistance by the female. For example, MacKinnon (1978) categorizes rape in orangutans as "aggressive intercourse" in which the females are struggling and screaming. Barash (1977) and Cox and LeBoeuf (1977) have used similar definitions concerning mallard ducks and elephant seals, respectively. The use of this type of definition is taken to an extreme by Janzen (1977). He suggests that "female" (seed-producing) parts of plants are raped by "male" (pollen-producing) parts of plants when the "males" force pollen into marginally receptive "females."

Most of these animal researchers emphasize that it is often difficult o draw the line between "coyness" and rape. (Sociobiologists use the term coyness to reflect female choosiness due to her larger investment in reproduction, based upon the view that eggs require more energy than do sperm). Symons (1979) says, "The primary difficulty in deciding whether a given copulation between members of a nonhuman animal species is 'really' rape is the same difficulty that jurors in rape trials often face: how can 'consent' be determined?" (p. 277). Further, these researchers have generally assumed that all sexual behavior involves persuasion by one partner, usually of the female by the male. "There is some element of female resistance implicit in all male-initiated courtship, otherwise the courtship would not be necessary. Moreover elements of male physical domination play a part in many a licit and mutually satisfactory seduction." (MacKinnon, 1978, p. 225). Heinroth (as cited by Lorenz, 1970) labelled the mating patterns he observed in the Egyptian goose as "prearranged mock rape" (p. 199) because the males vigorously pursued fleeing females. Cox and LeBoeuf (1977) went so far as to say the following, "Because of the way elephant-seal society is structured only a mature, high-ranking bull can rape a female . . . and it is such a male, who has demonstrated his fitness, that a female is selected to 'choose' to sire her offspring. Thus, it would benefit females to optimize the possibility of being raped!" (p. 329). Clearly such statements reinforce myths about rape. They create the idea that women may want to be raped and that a woman's verbal or physical refusal to engage in sex may actually mean that she is interested but is merely playing hard-to-get (the cliché, "your lips say no-no but there is yes-yes in your eyes").

Sexual behaviors which do not include the usual courtship displays seen in the species are often labelled as rape. For example, copulations in scorpionflies in which the male does not provide a nuptial offering to the female have also been called rape (Thornhill, 1980). Farr (1980) discusses rape in guppies as gonopodium thrusts with no display. Barash (1977) also used this type of definition in his work with mallards. He reported that unbonded, intruder males raped bonded females. This initial rape was characterized by a lack of courtship displaying by either the male or the female and by physical struggling by the female. In fact, the aggression was often so intense that the female drowned during the attempted rape. This was not the only rape that occurred, however. Following this violent rape by the intruder male, the female's bonded partner often raped her as well. Barash categorized this second copulation as rape because the usual mallard courtship displays were not seen. Interestingly, Bailey, Seymour, and Stewart (1978) found that while some of the "rape attempts" which they observed in blue-winged teal did not include courtship displays, other rape attempts did include displays by the male such as calling and head turns.

Some sociobiologists (e.g., Shields and Shields, 1983; Thornhill and Thornhill, 1983) have emphasized both increased fitness for the male rapists and decreased fitness of the female victim in their definition of rape. This type of approach can be seen in other situations as well. Fedigan (1982), using the example of infanticide, says that sociobiologists generally emphasize selection pressures on males. Female strategies are usually seen as losing to the more successful strategies employed by males.

Thornhill (1980) states that rape is, "forced insemination or fertilization" (p. 52). Interestingly, Barash (1977) emphasizes that animals should maximize their fitness but then defines rape as "any rape attempt in which mounting occurred, without regard to presumed success in transferring sperm" (p. 788). Further, as was pointed out by Hailman (1978) and McKinney, Barrett, and Derrickson (1978), the incidents Barash called rape often occurred when the animals were not fertile and the pairbonds were not stable. Also, Bailey et al (1978) reported that the forced mounting attempts which they observed in blue-winged teal were always unsuccessful.

Much of the research concerning forced and/or over aggressive sexual behavior in non-human primates indicates that such behaviors may not serve a reproductive purpose. MacKinnon (1978, 1979) suggests that rape in orangutans serves a social rather than reproductive function. Rijksen (1974) discussed those rapes as representing the establishment of dominance over females by subadult males. Galdikas (1979) viewed this behavior as a reproductive strategy of adolescent males since females always chose adult males with whom to mate. All of these researchers did report, however, that sexual encounters between estrus females and adult resident males did not involve force and that the sexual behavior was initiated by the female.

MacKinnon (1979) reported that the rate of pregnancy in orangutans following rape was lower than when the female initiated the sexual activity. He felt that this reflected the difficulty of two large orangutans successfully mating in trees without the willing participation of both animals. Nadler (1982a, 1982b) reported that when a male and female orangutan were housed together in a single cage, forced copulation by the male was frequent. When the animals were housed in a two compartment cage with a small door allowing access to one of the compartments only to the female due to her smaller size, the mating behavior was no longer aggressive. In the latter housing situation, females initiated the sexual activity and the rate of pregnancy was higher than in the situation where females were forced to copulate. It has also been reported that in pigtail monkeys (Eaton, 1973), rhesus monkeys (Herbert, 1968; Michael, Bonsall, and Zumpe, 1978) and chacma baboons (Saayman, 1970) females chose non-aggressive males as their sexual partners and did not choose aggressive males.

The sociobiological definitions of rape focus on forced, aggressive copulations which supposedly enhance a male's fitness. Contrary to this assertion, the animal data indicate that rapes are unsuccessful with regard to intromission and thus pregnancy. In fact, there has been no research which provides any empirical evidence that male animals who rape pass on their genes through rape.

The definitions of rape used in the animal literature by most sociobiologists center around three major points: the female must try to physically resist, intercourse and ejaculation must occur, and the male's reproductive fitness must improve. Not only has this definition failed to describe both human and other animal behavior, but the definition is frightening in its implications for human victims of rape. In many cases of rape, the victims feel that struggling will further endanger their lives and they therefore do not physically resist. Would the sociobiologists tell them that they had not been raped? Often victims are sodomized or forced to fellate their attackers. Would the sociobiologists tell them that they had not been raped? In some cases, forced intercourse does not end in ejaculation into the vagina. Would the sociobiologists tell the victim that she had not been raped? The vast majority of rapes do not lead to pregnancy, and many of the pregnancies which do result are aborted. Would the sociobiologists tell these women that they had not been raped? The reinforcement of rape myths (see Denmark and Friedman in this volume for an in depth discussion of the myths) is evident in the work of many sociobiologists. The above examples demonstrate the importance of defining the phenomenon of human rape as sexual behavior against a person's will.

It becomes clear that the sociobiological, historical, legal and feminist definitions of rape differ markedly. It is, therefore, imperative that the word rape be carefully and operationally defined when it is used. Further, use of the term should be avoided in ambiguous situations. For example, when a researcher sees what appears to be highly aggressive sexual behavior in a non-human species rather than labelling it as rape, it should be labelled merely as aggressive sexual behavior.

We are not suggesting that studying aggressive, forced sexual behavior in animals should be avoided. Certainly, it is important to examine such cases to more adequately understand sexual behavior. What is necessary, however, is great care in the use of highly charged terms such as rape, the avoidance of making statements about increased fitness which are unsubstantiated by data, and in generalizing from non-human behaviors to human behaviors.

REFERENCES

Abele, L. G., & Gilchrist, S. (1977). Homosexual rape and sexual selection in acanthocephalan worms. *Science, 197*, 81–83.

Alexander, R. D., & Noonan, K. M. (1979). Concealment of ovulation, parental care, and human social evolution. In N. A. Chagnon & W. Irons (Eds.), *Evolutionary biology and human social behavior: An anthropological perspective* (pp. 436–453). North Scituate, MA: Duxbury Press.

Bailey, R. O., Seymour, N. R., & Stewart, G. R. (1978). Rape behavior in blue-winged teal. *Auk, 95*, 188–190.

Barash, D. P. (1977). Sociobiology and rape in mallards (*Anas platyrhynchos*): Responses of the mated male. *Science, 197*, 788–789.

Barash, D. P. (1979). *The whisperings within*. New York: Harper & Row.

Bleier, R. (1984). *Science and gender: A critique of Biology and its theories on women*. New York: Pergamon Press.

Brownmiller, S. (1975). *Against our will: Men, women and rape*. New York: Simon and Schuster.

Calhoun, J. B. (1962). Population density and social pathology. *Scientific American, 206*, 139–148.

Caplan, A. L. (Ed.). (1978). *The sociobiology debate: Readings on ethical and scientific issues*. New York: Harper & Row.

Cox, C. R. and LeBoeuf, B. J. (1977). Female incitation of male competition: A mechanism in sexual selection. *The American Naturalist, 111*, 317–335.

Darwin, C. (1871). *The descent of man and selection in relation to sex*. London: John Murray.

Deutsch, H. (1944). *The psychology of women: Vol. I. Girlhood. New York:* Bantam Books.

Eaton, G. G. (1973). Social and endocrine determinants of sexual behavior in simian and prosimian females. In C. H. Phoenix (Ed.), *Primate reproductive behaviour* (Vol. 2). (pp. 20–35). Basel: S. Karger.

Farr, J. A. (1980). The effects of sexual experience and female receptivity on courtship-rape decisions in male guppies, *Poecilia reticulata (Pisces: Poeciliidae). Animal Behaviour, 28,* 1195–1201.

Fedigan, L. M. (1982). *Primate paradigms: Sex roles and social bonds.* Montreal: Eden Press.

Galdikas, B. (1979). Orangutan adaptation at Tanjung Puting Reserve: Mating and ecology. In D. A. Hamburg & E. R. McCown (Eds.), *The great apes* (pp. 195–233). Menlo Park, CA: Benjamin/Cummings.

Hailman, J. P. (1978). Rape among mallards. *Science, 201,* 280–281.

Herbert, J. (1968). Sexual preference in the rhesus monkey (*Macaca mulatta*) in the laboratory. *Animal Behaviour, 16,* 120–128.

Janzen, D. (1977). A note on optimal mate selection by plants. *The American Naturalist, 111,* 365–371.

Lewontin, R. C., Rose, S., & Kamin, L. J. (1984). *Not in our genes: Biology, ideology and human nature,* New York: Pantheon Books.

Lorenz, K. (1970). *Studies in animal and human behaviour,* Vol. I, Cambridge, MA: Harvard University Press.

Lorenz, K. (1971). *Studies in animal and human behaviour,* Vol. II. Cambridge, MA: Harvard University Press.

MacKinnon, J. (1978). *The ape within us.* New York: Holt, Rinehart & Winston.

MacKinnon, J. (1979). Reproductive behavior in wild orangutan populations. In D. A. Hamburg & E. R. McCown (Eds.), *The great apes* (pp. 257–273). Menlo Park, CA: Benjamin/Cummings.

McKinney, F., Barrett, J., & Derrickson, S. R. (1978). Rape among mallards. *Science, 201,* 281–282.

Meyer-Holzapfel, M. (1968). Abnormal behavior in zoo animals. In M. W. Fox (Ed.), *Abnormal behavior in animals.* Philadelphia: W. B. Saunders.

Michael, R. P., Bonsall, R. W., & Zumpe, D. (1978). Consort bonding and operant behavior by female rhesus monkeys. *Journal of Comparative and Physiological Psychology, 92,* 837–845.

Montagu, A. (Ed.) (1980). *Sociobiology examined.* Oxford: Oxford University Press.

Nadler, R. D. (1982a). Laboratory research on sexual behavior and reproduction of gorilla and orangutans. *American Journal of Primatology,* Suppl. 1, 57–66.

Nadler, R. D. (1982b). Reproductive behavior and endocrinology of orangutans. In L. E. M. De Bore (Ed.), *The Orang Utan: Its biology and conservation* (pp. 231–248). The Hague: Dr. W. Junk Publishers.

Parker, G. A. (1974). Courtship persistence and female-guarding as male time investment strategies. *Behaviour, 48,* 157–184.

Rijksen, H. D. (1974). Social structure in a wild orangutan population. *Proceedings of the sixth international congress of primatology.* London: Academic Press.

Rosoff, B. and Tobach, E. (Eds.). (1978–1985). *Genes and gender series* (Vols. I–V). New York: Gordian Press.

Saayman, G. S. (1970). The menstrual cycles and sexual behavior in a troop of free-ranging chacma baboons (*Papio ursinus*). *Folia Primatologica, 12,* 81–110.

Sahlins, M. (1976). *The use and abuse of biology: An anthropological critique of sociobiology.* Ann Arbor: The University of Michigan Press.

Shields, W. M. & Shields, L. M. (1983). Forcible rape: An evolutionary perspective. *Ethology and Sociobiology, 4,* 115–136.

Smith, R. I. (1968). The social aspects of reproductive behaviour in the Pintail. *Auk, 85,* 381–396.

Symons, D. (1979). *The evolution of human sexuality.* New York: Oxford University Press.

Thornhill, R. (1980). Rape in *Panorpa* scorpionflies and a general rape hypothesis. *Animal Behaviour, 28,* 52–59.

Thornhill, R. & Thornhill, N. W. (1983). Human rape: An evolutionary analysis. *Ethology and Sociobiology, 4,* 137–173.

Tinbergen, N. (1965). Some recent studies of the evolution of sexual behavior. In F. A. Beach (Ed.), *Sex and behavior* (pp. 1–33). New York: John Wiley & Sons, Inc.

Wilson, E. O. (1975). *Sociobiology: The new synthesis.* Cambridge, MA: The Belknap Press of Harvard University Press.

SOCIOBIOLOGICAL THEORY AND THE VIOLENT ABUSE OF WOMEN

Sarah Lenington

INSTITUTE OF ANIMAL BEHAVIOR
RUTGERS UNIVERSITY

Wilson published in 1975 the now classic book, *Sociobiology: The New Synthesis*, in which he reviewed the voluminous literature on the evolution of behavior of animals. In the last chapter of his book, he argued that human behavior has been subject to the same selection pressures as has been the behavior of other species. This final chapter engendered considerable criticism. It also inspired a rapidly growing body of literature on the evolution of human behavior, including publication during the past year of controversial papers on the topic of human rape (Shields and Shields, 1983; Thornhill and Thornhill, 1983).

The present chapter discusses the conceptual basis of the theory of evolution. In addition, it describes and criticizes some of the assumptions used in applying evolutionary theory to human behavior in general, and human rape in particular.

THE THEORY OF EVOLUTION

"Sociobiology" is the branch of behavioral biology that attempts to understand processes underlying the evolution of social behavior. The theory of evolution by natural selection was developed by Charles

Darwin in the mid 1800s. Darwin (1859) noted that all animals have the capacity to vastly overreproduce. For example, a single oyster sheds 100 million eggs each breeding season. If all those progeny survived, and each reproduced at the same rate, the world would quickly be covered with oysters. Even an animal that reproduced much more slowly, such as humans, is quite capable of covering the planet with members of its own species. However, with the fairly recent exception of humans, the world is not overpopulated with individuals of any species. The conclusion that was drawn from these observations is that the vast majority of individuals who are born do not reproduce. For example, if the number of oysters in the world is to stay constant, on average, only two of the progeny produced by an individual in its lifetime can reproduce. This means that each oyster produced hundreds of thousands of offspring that never breed.

Darwin assumed that most animals don't reproduce because they die before they ever get a chance to breed. He then reasoned that it may be that not all individuals of a species are alike. Individuals differ, and some of these differences may affect whether or not an individual ever reproduces. For example, some individuals may be better at avoiding predators than others. Individuals who were particularly good at avoiding predators would be more likely to survive long enough to breed. If the ability to avoid predators were genetically controlled, skill at avoiding predators could then be passed on to the progeny of those individuals who were able to reproduce. If most of the individuals who reproduced were good at avoiding predators, then, over time, most or all the individuals of that species would carry genes resulting in efficient predator avoidance.

This process, whereby individuals carrying particular genes are more likely to reproduce than are individuals possessing a different set of genes, is referred to as "natural selection." The characteristics of species produced by this differential reproduction (such as efficient predator avoidance) are referred to as "adaptations." Note that when a biologist claims that behavior is adaptive he or she means something quite different from what an anthropologist or psychologist might mean when using the same word. Adaptive behavior for a biologist does not necessarily lead to the survival of the group or species. It also does not necessarily lead to greater group cohesiveness or greater personal happiness. In a biological sense, all that is meant by adaptive behavior is that the behavior leads to greater reproductive success for the individual engaging in the behavior; i.e., individuals who engage in the behavior are more likely to reproduce or produce more offspring than they would if they behaved differently. The reason for this emphasis on reproduction is because it is only through reproduction that individuals pass on their genes.

During the past 20 years considerable attention has been directed toward understanding social behavior of animals in light of evolutionary theory. Social behavior of animals has been interpreted as consisting of strategies to maximize fitness (i.e., to maximize the number of young produced). Indeed, this research has been quite successful in shedding light on the adaptive nature of complex social interactions in animals. The success of sociobiology when applied to non-human animals has led investigators to hope that this approach might be equivalently fruitful when applied to humans.

THEORETICAL ASSUMPTIONS OF HUMAN SOCIOBIOLOGY

In general, there are three ways in which inferences are made about the evolution or adaptiveness of human behavior. The first is to reconstruct the probable life style and ecology of our hominid ancestors and try to figure out what selection pressures may have existed, 25,000 years ago, 500,000 years ago, or 3.5 million years ago. Behavior of humans today is then interpreted as an outcome of selection pressures in the remote past. This was the approach taken by Wilson in his book but the approach has some obvious drawbacks. It is hard enough to determine what selection pressures are existing today on animal populations we can observe. The problems facing anyone trying to determine what selection pressures existed for creatures we will never see, living in an ecological setting we have never experienced, are formidable.

A second approach is to examine currently existing cultures and look for universals in human behavior (Daly and Wilson, 1978; Eibl-Eibesfeldt, 1970). These "universal traits" are then assumed to have a genetic basis and to be the product of natural selection. However, even a cursory examination of the anthropological literature indicates that there are very few universals in human behavior. If human behavior can be characterized at all, it is noteworthy for its variety and plasticity.

A further drawback of these first two lines of reasoning is that they both assume that there has been selection for specific behaviors during the course of evolution, and that these behaviors are "genetically programmed." Not only does this fly in the face of everything that is understood by psychologists and anthropologists about the importance of learning and culture in human behavior, but it even flies in the face of what is known about the genetic control of behavior. There is little agreement about the genetic control of human behavior since the genetics of human behavior is a topic that is notoriously difficult to study. However, the genetic control of behavior of some non-human animals has been well studied and even the behavior of relatively simple (when compared to humans) animals such as mice is not rigidly "genetically programmed." Even in mice, there is no such thing as a gene for aggression or a gene for nest-building, or a gene for any other specific behavior. For example, aggressive behavior in mice is affected not only by the presence of a large number of genes but also is affected by the genetic background of the mouse and many environmental factors. This complex nature of genetic influences on behavior of creatures such as mice, renders absurd any theory of human behavior that supposes a simple relationship between genes and behavior in humans. Indeed, some of the harshest criticism of sociobiology has come from geneticists themselves (Lewontin, 1979).

A third approach to the evolution of human behavior attempts to avoid some of these pitfalls (Irons, 1979a; Alexander, 1979). Stated in most general terms, this approach argues that in humans (as well as in many other animals) there has not been selection for specific behaviors at all. Rather there has been selection for a decision making process that tends to reach biologically adaptive conclusions. This theory argues that the effect of selection has been to regulate cognitive processes and emotional reactions in biologically adaptive ways. According to this theory individuals who behave differently do not necessarily differ genetically, but simply differ in environmental circumstances. This then leads them to adopt differing behavioral strategies each of which may be adaptive for a particular environment. Therefore, rather than there being selection for particular behaviors in humans, there has been selection for plasticity of behavior.

Use of this approach often entails comparing human behavior with that of other species of animals. Although the extreme plasticity of human behavior is unprecedented in the animal kingdom, adaptive changes in behavior of other species are commonly observed when ecological conditions change. Thus practitioners of this method, those who are interested in a particular human behavior, be it altruism, maternal behavior, child abuse, rape, murder, or any of a number of other behaviors, look for examples of these behaviors in non-human species. The researchers attempt to determine under what conditions the behaviors occur, and then they examine these behaviors in humans to determine whether or not the behaviors occur under the same circumstances. If the circumstances are the same, the behaviors are pronounced adaptive. The recent attempts to interpret human rape in evolutionary terms have taken this approach. This approach is not without its own pitfalls. However, before I address some of the limitations of this approach, I would like to outline the theoretical arguments used to claim that rape may be a biologically adaptive behavior.

SOCIOBIOLOGICAL THEORY AND HUMAN RAPE

Theories about rape derive from a theory Darwin used to explain differences in reproductive behavior between males and females. Darwin (1871) noted that males and females differed enormously in the number of young they could potentially produce. He argued that sperm is virtually unlimited in supply and takes little energy to make. Eggs, on the other hand, are far fewer in number and physiologically more expensive to produce. One consequence of this disparity in the numbers and kinds of gametes produced, is that if a male mates with a genetically unfit female all he has lost is a few minutes of his time, whereas if a female mates with an unfit male she wastes one of her eggs and, furthermore, if she is a mammal she may commit herself to a lengthy and physiologically draining pregnancy. Therefore, Darwin argued that it would be adaptive for females to be much more choosey than males when it came to picking a mate. Females should assess males not only for their genetic qualities, but if males continued to associate with females after copulation, females should also assess males with respect to the resources males could provide. Some resources provided by a male, such as food for females or young, or nest-sites that are safe from predators, may be very important components determining how many young are raised.

Darwin also argued that selection should not only favor males being less choosey about their mates than females, but also that selection should favor males attempting to copulate with as many females as possible. Thus it has been postulated that there is a basic conflict between males and females regarding optimal reproductive strategies.

In some animal species producing young entails no investment on the part of males other than the time and energy necessary for copulation. However, in humans and many other species, production of young requires a considerable investment of time and resources on the part of both males and females. In species where males participate in parental care, the ideal mate from a female's point of view will be monogamous and devote all his time and energy to providing resources for herself and their young. However, this may not be the optimal strategy for a male, since he might produce more offspring if he copulated with other females. This conflict in sexual strategies may therefore produce behaviors in each sex which are viewed as highly undesirable by members of the opposite sex.

It has been proposed in the recent papers by Thornhill and Thornhill (1983) and Shields and Shields (1983) that men have three strategies whereby they can produce young. The first is honest courtship in which the man fully intends to raise young with the woman. The second is deceptive courtship whereby a man attempts to convince the woman that he will raise young with her, but in reality has no intention of doing so and leaves after copulation. The final strategy, made possible by the greater size and strength of men as compared with women, is to force a woman to copulate, i.e., rape. Although the authors of these papers argue that all men are capable of pursuing all three strategies, which one is adopted will depend on the relative costs and benefits for any individual man. For a man to be able to pursue the first two strategies, he must be able to attract a mate. Furthermore, if he is to honestly court a woman he must have the economic resources to make raising a child feasible. If a man lacks resources necessary for child rearing *and* does not have the potential to attract a desirable mate, he may turn to rape as an alternative mode of producing young. Viewed from this perspective then, rape in humans is primarily a reproductive strategy, rather than an aggressive strategy; a strategy that is employed primarily by men who are unable to compete successfully for mates and resources. The principal evidence presented for claiming that rape is primarily a reproductive strategy is the age distribution of the victims. The majority of rape victims are women in their prime reproductive years. The age distribution of these women differs markedly from the age distribution of victims of other violent crimes such as murder. The main evidence used to claim that men rape when they are unable to produce children through more conventional means is the age and socioeconomic status of rapists. Rapists tend to be young, poor men. Such men are assumed by the authors to be less able to raise families than would older, more affluent men. Since rapes do sometimes result in pregnancy, these papers argue that these "low quality" men who rape have a higher fitness than they would if they did not force women to copulate.

PROBLEMS IN SOCIOBIOLOGICAL ANALYSES OF HUMAN BEHAVIOR

The best sociobiological studies of animal behavior have documented the relationship between behavior and fitness, measuring the number of young produced by individuals pursuing various behavioral strategies. Only a handful of studies on the evolution of human behavior have been able to also look at the consequences of behavior for fitness (for example: Chagnon, 1979; Irons, 1979b). These few papers on humans are all anthropological studies, carried out in non-industrialized societies. The bulk of the research on human sociobiology bases its conclusions on plausibility and analogies with the behavior of animals. If a plausible story can be concocted to account for selection for the behavior, and if some other animal species behaves similarly under comparable circumstances, the behavior is pronounced adaptive. However, what is plausible is very much in the eye of the beholder. The problems that can be generated by this approach are illustrated by a story that perfectly exemplifies the dilemma confronting all sociobiologists who substitute plausibility for evidence. The story has enjoyed great vogue among evolutionary biologists although it is probably apocryphal. The story involves a conversation between a professor and his graduate student. The graduate student was describing his thesis research in which he was studying the reactions of mice to predators. He was studying two populations of mice, one living in fields and one living in woods. The graduate student explained that when a predator appeared, the mice living in woods would flee, whereas the mice living in fields froze. The professor thought for a moment and said "Oh! That makes perfect sense. In woods there are lots of logs and other places for a mouse to hide so of course in woods they would run for a refuge. But in fields, it is not as easy to find a hiding place. Therefore it would be more adaptive for a field mouse to freeze."

"Oh, I'm sorry" interrupted the student. "I got it all backwards. It's the mice in the fields who flee and the mice in the woods who freeze."

"But of course!" said the professor. "After all, the pattern of light and shade in the woods would make a mouse who froze be cryptic, but mice out in the open would be more visible, so it would be much more adaptive for mice in fields to run for their burrows."

In short, the extent of human plasticity is rivaled only by the extent of human ingenuity. As long as we rely on plausibility arguments, anything can be made to seem adaptive. Although it may be plausible that men who lack resources to raise a family may turn to rape as a way of increasing their reproductive output, it would be just as plausible to argue that only wealthy men should be rapists, since only wealthy men might have time and energy necessary to pursue multiple women.

Unfortunately, the authors of papers on rape also pay little attention to data that are contrary to their theory. Although they argue that men who rape do so because they are unable to obtain mates by more con entional means, in reality a large percentage of rapists are married. Although this fact is noted in the paper by Thornhill and Thornhill (1983), it is dismissed by suggesting that these married rapists do not have what they perceive to be "suitable mates" (p. 164). However, the divorce rate in the United States would suggest that a very large number of men do not feel they have "suitable mates," yet the vast majority of these men are not rapists. The large number of married rapists poses a serious problem for the theory advocated in these two papers. Its casual dismissal by Thornhill and Thornhill and absence of any reference to the phenomenon by Shields and Shields (1983) indicates a considerably greater commitment on the part of the authors to a plausible theory than to data.

A second problem with these papers concerns use of evolutionary theory to explain "deviant" behavior in twentieth century industrialized cultures. Patterns of human behavior in modern technological societies in many instances are completely the opposite of those predicted by evolutionary theory. For example, evolutionary theory predicts large family size under conditions of resource abundance and small families when resources are scarce; yet among humans in twentieth century industrial cultures the reverse pattern is found (Lande, 1978). Technological societies have confronted humans with a social environment unprecedented in our evolutionary history (vast numbers of people living in extremely dense concentrations, high mobility, diminished ties between kin). Our behavior under such circumstances may be no more biologically adaptive than that of overcrowded animals living in a zoo. Furthermore, culturally deviant behavior may not be the best subject for studying the evolution of human behavior. If a biologist picked a behavior that for example only one in 1000 chimpanzees ever engaged in and tried to spin an elaborate story about the adaptive significance of the behavior, he or she would never be taken seriously. Sociobiological analyses of animal behavior are based on normative behavior patterns of the species or population. If an unusual behavior pattern is seen it may be interpreted as individual idiosyncrasy but not as having adaptive significance. As humans we are understandably fascinated with deviant behavior because it seems dramatic and fear of such behavior often has a powerful effect on our lives. However, in a given year the probability of being raped is .003 for a white woman, .02 for a black woman, and .007 for a chicano woman (Sanford et al., 1979 cited in Thornhill and Thornhill, 1983). Behaviors that occur at such a low rate are probably far more informative about the individual pathology of the actor, than about the evolutionary history of the species.

Many of the above criticisms do not apply solely to the recent papers on rape, but are also applicable to sociobiological analyses of other deviant behavior (e.g., Daly and Wilson, 1978, 1981; Lightcap, Kurland and Burgess, 1982) in western society (including my own previous work on child abuse (Lenington, 1981). The whole sorry history of the misuse of biological research in formulating political and social policy indicates that biological explanations of such behavior can be used to either label the individual engaging in such behavior as "genetically inferior" or alternatively, to excuse such behavior on the grounds that it is "natural." It would be most unfortunate if any papers on human sociobiology (and particularly ones based on such shaky scientific evidence) were used for either purpose.

REFERENCES

Alexander, R. D. (1979). Evolution and culture. In N. A. Chagnon and W. Irons (Eds.), *Evolutionary biology and human social behavior* (pp. 59–78). North Scituate, MA: Duxbury Press.

Chagnon, N. A. (1979). Is reproductive success equal in egalitarian societies? In N. A. Chagnon and W. Irons (Eds.), *Evolutionary biology and human social behavior* (pp. 374–401). North Scituate, MA: Duxbury Press.

Daly, M. and Wilson, M. (1978). *Sex, evolution and behavior.* North Scituate, MA: Duxbury Press.

Daly, M. and Wilson, M. (1981). Child maltreatment from an evolutionary perspective. *New Directions in Child Development, 11,* 93–112.

Darwin, C. (1859). *On the origin of species by means of natural selection; or The preservation of favoured races in the struggle for life.* London: John Murray.

Darwin, C. (1871). *The descent of man and selection in relation to sex:* London: John Murray.

Eibl-Eibesfeldt, I. (1970). *Ethology: The biology of behavior.* New York: Holt, Rinehart, and Winston.

Irons, W. (1979a). Natural selection, adaptation, and human social behavior. In N. A. Chagnon and W. Irons (Eds.), *Evolutionary biology and human social behavior* (pp. 4–38), North Scituate, MA: Duxbury Press.

Irons, W. (1979b). Cultural and biological success. In N. A. Chagnon and W. Irons (Eds.), *Evolutionary biology and human social behavior* (pp. 257–272). North Scituate, MA: Duxbury Press.

Lande, R. (1978). Are humans maximizing reproductive success? *Behavioral Ecology and Sociobiology, 3,* 95–98.

Lenington, S. (1981). Child abuse: The limits of sociobiology. *Ethology and Sociobiology, 2,* 17–29.

Lewontin, R. C. (1979). Sociobiology as an adaptationist program. *Behavioral Science, 24,* 5–14.

Lightcap, J. L., Kurland, J. A., and Burgess, R. L. (1982). Child abuse: A test of some predictions from evolutionary theory. *Ethology and Sociobiology, 3,* 61–67.

Shields, W. M. and Shields, L. M. (1983). Forcible rape: An evolutionary perspective. *Ethology and Sociobiology, 4,* 115–136.

Thornhill, R. and Thornhill, N. W. (1983). Human rape: An evolutionary analysis. *Ethology and Sociobiology, 4,* 137–173.

Wilson, E. O. (1975). *Sociobiology: The new synthesis.* Cambridge, MA: Harvard University Press.

SOCIOBIOLOGICAL HYPOTHESES ABOUT RAPE: A CRITICAL LOOK AT THE DATA BEHIND THE HYPOTHESES

Cheryl F. Harding

HUNTER COLLEGE, AND
DEPARTMENT OF ORNITHOLOGY
AMERICAN MUSEUM OF NATURAL HISTORY

INTRODUCTION

"Sociobiology is defined as the systematic study of the biological basis of all social behavior" (Wilson, 1975, p. 4). Its proponents see sociobiology as a comparative science which derives its information from comparison of the thousands of species which have evolved some form of sociality. According to E.O. Wilson, its primary synthesizer and founder, "The purpose of sociobiology is not to make crude comparisons between animal species or between animals and men, for example simply to compare warfare and animal aggression or slavery in ants as opposed to men. Its purpose is to develop general laws of the evolution and biology of social behavior, which might then be extended in a disinterested manner to the study of human beings" (Wilson in Barash, 1977, p. xiv). The purpose of the present chapter is to examine hypotheses some sociobiologists have developed about the occurrence of rape in human populations. These sociobiological, evolutionary hypotheses see rape as a potentially adaptive behavior rather than one which is necessarily pathological (Shields and Shields, 1983). They are based on comparative data from a variety of species in which sociobiologists have reported rape behavior to occur. The occurrence of rape in nonhuman species is a crucial point for the development of these hypotheses, and one which is open to question.

When Susan Brownmiller wrote her analysis of rape in 1975, she stated that rape was a uniquely human behavior; to the best of her knowledge, no zoologist had claimed to observe the occurrence of rape among animals in their natural habitats. In the years since her book was published, many sociobiologists have reported the occurrence of what they describe as rape, forced copulation or stolen fertilization in a variety of animals including insects (e.g., Manning, 1967; Thornhill, 1980), fishes (e.g. Barlow, 1967; Farr, 1980; Keenleyside, 1972; Kodric-Brown, 1977), amphibians (e.g., Howard, 1978; Wells, 1977), birds (e.g., Barash, 1977; Beecher and Beecher, 1979; McKinney, Barrett and Derrickson, 1978; Mineau and Cooke, 1979), mammals (e.g., Cox and LeBoeuf, 1977), and nonhuman primates (e.g., Galdikas, 1979; MacKinnon, 1974, 1979). Some of these references predate Brownmiller's book. These few references do not call Brownmiller's knowledge of the literature to question. It was not until sociobiologists searched the literature for any instance of animal behavior which could possibly be construed as rape that these instances were particularly noted. In some cases, the original authors had not mentioned the term rape in their description of the behavior in question, but other researchers decided that the behavior described could be interpreted as rape. These workers suggest that since rape occurs across such a wide variety of species, biological models of rape behavior should provide valuable insight into its causation and possibly its control in human populations. Others have pointed out that just because a particular behavior such as rape is found in many cultures or across many species does not necessarily imply that it is genetically determined and therefore subject to biological explanation (Silverberg, 1980). But does rape occur in animals?

THE DEFINITION OF RAPE

The first problem confronting the scientist who wishes to study rape is to define the term. The term rape has a multitude of meanings, depending upon its usage. While different usages may share a common core meaning, the precise definition may vary a great deal. In the most general sense, rape is defined as a sexual act forced on an individual against its will. Specific definitions of rape vary from one scientific study to another. Studies of rape in human populations usually utilize the current legal definition of rape, but even this varies. In the United States, most states define rape as "an act of sexual intercourse with a female, not one's wife, against her will and consent, whether her will is overcome by force or fear of force. . . ." (Brownmiller, 1975, p. 368). Thus, in most states, only a sexual act forced on a woman by a man constitutes rape, but in some states, the definition of rape has been extended to include forced homosexual acts or sexual acts forced on men by women. While all states consider forced vaginal intercourse to be rape, they differ in whether other sexual acts are also considered to constitute rape, and if so, which particular acts are covered under rape statutes. There is also variation in whether intercourse forced on a wife by her husband is considered rape. As can be seen from the definition of rape given above, in most states such an act is not considered rape; in these states, a woman gives up her legal right to refuse intercourse with her husband when she marries. Examination of the definitions of rape in other cultures also reveals great variation. Thus, even when confining the discussion of rape to the human case, there is variation in how the term is used and what it means.

Applying the term rape to animal behavior is even more problematic. Sociobiologists appear to be interested in the occurrence of rape among nonhuman animals because they would like to develop a general model which could explain the occurrence of rape behavior in all species, including humans. When we see an article such as "Rape in the lesser snow goose" (Mineau and Cooke, 1979), we generally assume that the authors are describing a behavior in geese which is similar to human rape behavior. This may or may not be the case. When sociobiologists apply the term rape to nonhuman animals, they usually are not using it in the same sense that we do when we speak about human behavior. They are not using the same legal definitions, and they are using the term in very different circumstances from the common usage with which we are all familiar. Sociobiologists have applied the term rape to a variety of animal behaviors, some of which bear a superficial resemblance to rape as defined in humans, and others which show no resemblance at all. For example, mating behavior in elephant seals, in which the larger male often appears to force sexual attentions on the smaller female, using his large mass to pin the female down to prevent escape (Cox and LeBoeuf, 1977), appears to be force on the part of the perpetrator and resistance by the victim which we associate with acts of rape in humans. However, many acts termed rape in other species involve no overt resistance on the part of the female (e.g., Beecher and Beecher, 1979; Mineau and Cooke, 1979), and therefore no evidence that the act is against her will. Describing such acts as rape seems questionable. One of the most bizarre uses of the term involves externally fertilizing species such as fish, in which the intrusion of a male into another male's nest while the latter is fertilizing a female's eggs has been described as rape or rape-like behavior (e.g., see discussion of Keenleyside, 1972 beginning on p. 30). Such behavior would seem totally unrelated to human rape behavior. Applying the term rape to the behavior of nonhuman animals causes a number of semantic and theoretical difficulties. (Problems particular to specific cases will be discussed later.) In all cases, it implies a similarity in the form of animal and human behavior which often does not exist. Beyond this, applying the term rape to nonhuman behavior also suggests a similarity between nonhuman animals and humans in the motivation underlying such behavior and in its adaptive value before such similarities have been demonstrated.

Sociobiologists who use anthropomorphic terms such as rape, cuckoldry and adultery to describe animal behavior have departed from the generally accepted practice of ethologists and comparative psychologists of using neutral terms to describe behavior patterns. Scientists in the latter disciplines are trained to rigorously exclude anthropomorphic terms to describe animal behavior, because anthropomorphic terms tends to impute functions to behavior which have not been demonstrated, and may prevent the scientist from correctly interpreting the function and/or the underlying motivation of a particular behavior pattern (see Marler and Hamilton, 1966). The argument has often been made that the choice of words and analogies critically affects our evaluation of data. The use of metaphor in scientific analysis can become so central to the way we view a problem that the metaphor itself serves as an implicit conceptual framework (see Beer, 1983). As Beach stated, "Language is more than a tool for describing the world. It is a means of *creating* the world." (1979, p. 98) There is no understanding a phenomenon independent of the language used to describe it. The term rape in particular is loaded with emotional associations, moral and ethical connotations which are difficult to ignore. Legal scholars even suggest that the term rape should no longer be used to describe human behavior because of the negative connotations this word directs toward the victim in our culture. They suggest instead the use of less emotionally loaded terms, such as sexual assault, sexual battery or criminal sexual conduct (Offir, 1982). Often sociobiologists who use anthropomorphic terms claim to disavow the common associations and connotations of these words; however, their sincerity is somewhat suspect. Sociobiologists expect people to dissociate the term rape from all its common meanings and associations. And if such dissociation is what they truly desire, then why do they not develop some alternative neutral terminology to describe the behavior as other scientists strive to do?

Another problem in applying the term rape to animal behavior, is that it implies that scientists understand the motivation and the sexual preferences of the animal they are describing as the rape victim — that scientists can unequivocally determine when an animal is resisting the sexual advances of another animal and when it is not (Estep and Bruce, 1981). This is more problematic than it might at first seem. Resistance by the female is one of the defining characteristics of rape in humans, but protracted resistance of male mating attempts is a normal part of female sexual behavior in some species. For example, in their study of elephant seals, Cox and LeBoeuf (1977) found that female seals routinely resisted male mounting attempts. Mating in this species has often been described as rape. Male elephant seals show no overt courtship behavior prior to mounting, and females show no active solicitation. Females strongly resist male mating attempts, but the much larger males appear to overpower the females. Of the 1478 mounts which Cox and LeBoeuf observed, 79% were vigorously resisted by the female until the male dismounted or, on rare occasions, achieved intromission, and 13.7% were resisted when the male first mounted, but the female ceased protesting before the male intromitted or dismounted. Only 7.3% of male mounts were not resisted by the females. If only mounting attempts directed at females known to be in estrus (i.e., here defined as the period between the first and last observed copulation) are considered, estrous females totally resisted 62.7% of all mounts, initially resisted 24.4%, and did not resist only 12.9% of mounts. The authors suggested that this behavior which looks like rejection is really a female strategy to test and compare males. By protesting mounting attempts, females incite interference by higher ranking males, and only high-ranking males will be able to continue their mating attempts without being interrupted by other males. Female resistance was, in fact, correlated with increased interference by nearby males. Twenty-five percent of unresisted mounts were interrupted by neighboring males, but 61.4% of totally resisted mounts were interrupted. Resisting increased the probability that a mount would be interrupted by the most dominant male in the vicinity and that the female would mate with him. Obviously, prolonged female resistance is a normal part of mating behavior in this species. If a female initially resists mating attempts by a male, but ultimately mates with him, how is a scientist to decide if this is a forced mating in which the male finally overpowered the female or if the male's prolonged attempt changed the female's motivational state so that in the end she copulated willingly? Decisions as to whether to classify such a mating as forced or willing are based as much on the theoretical orientation of the scientists as on the behavior of the animals involved. Thus, what one scientist describes as rape, appears to another to be a female strategy to induce male competition.

WHEN SOCIOBIOLOGISTS SAY RAPE, WHAT DO THEY MEAN?

As pointed out by Estep and Bruce (1981), scientists working with animal data have tended to use the term rape in two ways. The first is not to define the term at all. This is found both in descriptive studies and in theoretical reviews. Many authors of descriptive studies never explicitly define the behavior they consider to constitute rape in the animals they are observing (e.g., Manning, 1967; Beecher and Beecher, 1979; Power and Doner, 1980). A careful reading of their articles, helps one to develop some sense of how the term rape is being used, and often it is very different from what one would expect from the common meaning of the word (i.e., a sexual act forced on an individual against its will). This is discussed further in the next section on redefinition. In theoretical articles, authors rarely give explicit operational definitions of what they mean when they use the term rape or how the word has been used in the various studies they review. Thus, theoretical generalizations are often based on non-equivalent data, because the various researchers who collected the descriptive data defined rape differently. In some cases, the original authors did not even mention rape, but later workers decided that the behavior described met their definition of rape, and then they go on to cite these studies as evidence of rape behavior in various species. However, the way to learn this is by consulting the original articles. Sociobiologists' claims about the widespread occurrence of rape in the animal world (e.g., Shields and Shields, 1983 or Thornhill and Thornhill, 1983) would be much less impressive if it were immediately obvious how rape was defined in the various studies cited as documenting the occurrence of rape.

The second tendency is for scientists to redefine rape in specialized ways to suit the particular problem on which they are working. The most common redefinition of rape in animal studies involves applying the term rape to male-female interactions in which the authors give no indication that the females are actually resisting the sexual behavior of the males. In most species, copulation is usually preceded by extensive courtship displays by the males and active solicitation displays by the female. When a male and female copulate without engaging in precopulatory displays, this has been called rape by some scientists although there is no evidence of resistance on the female's part and rarely is there evidence that the male used force. Such redefinition may be explicit as in Mineau and Cooke (1979) or implicit as in Beecher and Beecher (1979) or Farr (1980). Yet, in animal studies, female resistance would seem to be the primary measure by which a human observer could attempt to judge whether a copulation was forced on a female by a male. As discussed previously, this is not to suggest it is easy to determine when females are resisting and when they are not, but if one wants to generalize from animals to the human condition, the animal studies should at least be examining something which approximates human rape behavior.

Instead, animal studies often examine quite different behavior and call it rape. These data are then used to hypothesize about human rape behavior. For example, several avian studies have presented dead female models to reproductively active birds in the field (e.g., Butler, 1982; Hoogland and Sherman, 1976; Weatherhead and Robertson, 1980). The models are usually presented in a horizontal posture which presumably resembles the normal female copulation solicitation posture in these species. The tendency of males to mount and attempt to copulate with such models is given as a measure of males tendency to rape. But since the models cannot resist male copulation attempts, and in fact are posed in a manner which might tend to solicit such attempts, such behavior would seem to have little bearing on rape behavior as it is usually defined.

The term rape has also been used to describe the behavior of animals such as fish in which fertilization occurs externally (e.g., Barlow, 167; Keenleyside, 1972; Kodric-Brown, 1977). I should like to point out that this is an instance in which the original authors did not describe the behavior as rape, but Shields and Shields (1983) listed these studies as evidence for the occurrence of rape in fishes in their theoretical review of forcible rape. Shields and Shields did hedge somewhat by stating that the studies listed were evidence of "behavior interpreted as forced copulation, stolen fertilization, or explicitly as rape. . ." (1983, p. 116). However, the reader is left with the impression that rape behavior has been observed in a wide variety of animals from invertebrates to man. But, is it reasonable to describe the behavior of these fish as rape? Keenleyside described the northern longear sunfish, stating that males dig small, bowl-shaped nests in the substrate. Male nests are usually grouped closely together, and each male defends his small nest scrape against conspecific males. Females enter the nest colony to spawn. A female enters a male's territory, and the two begin to circle slowly in the nest scrape. Their spawning behavior is often interrupted by the intrusion of other males, sometimes neighboring territory holders, sometimes young males without territories. These males appear to be entering the nest when the female releases eggs. The territorial male usually chases the intruder away and then resumes spawning. Keenleyside states that these disruptive intrusions occur repeatedly, and he observed up to 30 intrusions into one nest during a five minute period at the height of the spawning season. Although he had no conclusive evidence, the intruders appeared to be releasing sperm and attempting to fertilize the females' eggs themselves. Thus, so called rape behavior in the longear sunfish does not involve any contact between rapist and victim, merely possible fertilization of a female's eggs by a male she may not have chosen to mate with. Similar behavior was described in the pupfish (Kodric-Brown, 1977) and a South American leaf fish (Barlow, 1967). An interesting twist in the case of the leaf fish was that intruding males would often mimic the coloration and behavior of females to gain access to the male's nest while a female was spawning. In none of these cases was there any indication that females ever resisted the intrusion of these males or that spawning females ever left their spawning sites because of the intrusion of conspecific males. Thus, categorizing this behavior as rape appears to be a somewhat bizarre redefinition of the term, and one which has very little bearing on the occurrence of rape in humans.

Other researchers actually suggest that female animals not only do not necessarily resist rape attempts but that they may actually "'welcome' some rapes," because they may increase the genetic diversity of their offspring (Mineau and Cooke, 1981, p. 289). Calling it rape in copulations where no resistance is observed seems highly questionable and certainly a departure from the definition of rape in human populations. Generalizing from such cases to cases of human rape in which the victim does resist would also seem improper. This is an important issue which is often ignored. In many instances, the criteria which sociogiologists use to define rape in animal and human populations appear to be different, but this difference is never explicitly discussed. One is left to infer such differences from careful reading of descriptive studies and from statements as "Rape . . . at least in humans is against her will." (Shields and Shields, 1983, p. 119).

Certain sociobiologists have gone even further in redefining rape in an attempt to explain the adaptive value of rape and the particular motivation which may cause males to rape. The most extreme example is Thornhill and Thornhill (1983). These authors redefine rape to describe only those instances of forced sexual behavior which might result in the fertilization of eggs. In addition, they specify that such behavior must enhance the fitness of the male involved while decreasing the fitness of the female. This is a much more limited definition of rape than that in common use, and according to this definition, many acts which meet current legal definitions of rape are not considered to be rape by the Thornhills. For example, under the Thornhills' definition, an attack against a woman past menopause is not rape because this act cannot result in fertilization. Similarly, under this definition, sexual assaults involving sodomy or fellatio are not rape, though they are considered such under some criminal statutes. Even a case of sexual assault which resulted in pregnancy, the victim is not considered to be raped unless it can be shown that this pregnancy has somehow lowered the victim's fitness (i.e., decrease the number of descendants she will produce). Presumably, if a man sexually assaulted a nun and she became pregnant, the Thornhills would not consider it rape because the rapist had in fact increased the nun's fitness, since she probably had no intention of having children. It is impossible to determine to what extent being raped lowers a woman's fitness. One common example given to illustrate how rape might lower a woman's fitness is that the rapist has lower-quality genes than the woman's spouse, so the resulting offspring will be of lower quality than any she might conceive with her husband. A second example often given is that the fact that a woman has been raped makes it difficult for her to attract a suitable husband and obtain his help to raise the large family which she had presumably planned. Of course, objectively determining the "quality" of one man's genes versus another's poses an insurmountable problem, as does determining what a woman would have done with her life if she had not been raped. Sociobiologists have often been criticized for setting up hypotheses like these which cannot be empirically tested. In any case, it is clear that the common legal definitions of rape and those used by sociobiologists whether referring to human or nonhuman behavior, are often very different.

For reasons documented in the foregoing discussion of the problems of semantics and definition, I think using the term rape to describe the behavior of animals is inappropriate. Many researchers create further semantic problems by using the term rape to mean different things at different points in their writing, switching from common usage to legal definitions, to specialized definitions without warning. Applying the term rape to animal behavior is imprecise, sensationalistic and disguises the fact that when researchers apply the term to animal behavior, what they are describing is usually something quite different from rape behavior as it occurs in humans. It also leads people to assume that behavior described as rape in animals has the same form, the same function and the same adaptive value as rape behavior in humans when in fact none of these things have been demonstrated. It also leads one to attribute human moral values to animal behavior. Alternative, more neutral descriptive terms should be used to facilitate scientific inquiry. Two of the terms which have been suggested are forced copulation or resisted mating.

DOES BEHAVIOR ANALOGOUS TO RAPE OCCUR IN ANIMALS?

It is quite clear that behaviors analogous to rape are not as widespread among animals as some sociobiologists would lead us to believe. A large number of the examples cited as demonstrating the existence of rape in a variety of species may be dismissed because there is no evidence that females resisted mating attempts described as rapes (e.g., Barlow, 1967; Beecher and Beecher, 1979; Farr, 1980;

Howard, 1978; Keenleyside, 1972; Kodric-Brown, 1977; Mineau and Cooke, 1979; Wells, 1977). Some studies did mention sporadic resistance by some females, but female resistance was not a defining characteristic of the behavior patterns described as rape. In other cases, the behavior described was directed toward stuffed models of females. These models, of course, could not resist the copulation attempts of males and actually were posed in what would appear to be solicitation postures which would invite male sexual advances (e.g., Butler, 1982; Hoogland and Sherman, 1976; Weatherhead and Robertson, 1980). So these studies also give no evidence of rape behavior.

The best evidence for behavior resembling rape comes from work on insects and dabbling ducks. Rape-like behavior involving the use of force by the male and documented resistance on the part of the female has been described in two genera of flies, *Drosophila* (Manning, 1967) and *Panorpa* (Thornhill, 1980) and 39 species of dabbling ducks (McKinney, et al., 1983). Maintaining captive populations of these species in crowded quarters with little or no cover and giving females little or no chance of avoiding the advances of males increases the frequency with which forced copulations are observed (Manning, 1967; McKinney, et al., 1983). McKinney stresses that one must be very careful in classifying copulations as forced, since female resistance and escape are a normal part of courtship and copulation sequences in mated pairs in the various species of ducks he has observed. Another similarity to human rape behavior is that female ducks which are the victims of forced copulations, often by large groups of males, may sustain serious injury or even be killed during these interactions (McKinney, et al., 1983).

Data on apparent forced copulation in mammals other than humans are rare. Sociobiologists have cited Cox and LeBoeuf's work on the elephant seal (1977) as evidence that rape is common in this species, but as described above, prolonged female resistance is a normal part of mating in this species. Therefore, reasonable scientists differ on whether behavior of the elephant seal should be characterized as analogous to human rape. Despite extensive observation of a large variety of nonhuman primates, behavior resembling human rape has only been described for one species, the orangutan (Fedigan, 1982). Forced copulations are described as the occasional acts of primarily adolescent males directed toward females which would not normally mate with them (Galdikas, 1979; MacKinnon, 1974, 1979). It is suggested that males can achieve intromission only if females show some degree of cooperation (MacKinnon, 1979). Of course, if the females are cooperating, this raises the question of whether it is reasonable to describe such behavior as rape.

These data illustrate that the occurrence of rape-like behavior is not nearly as widespread in the animal kingdom as some sociobiologists would have us believe. Rather than being a common male reproductive strategy found in many species from invertebrates to primates, it appears to be an uncommon behavior which occurs in a few isolated species. There is no broad database across phyla on which to found hypotheses of male sexual selection for rape.

SOCIOBIOLOGY AND THE PROBLEM OF ULTIMATE CAUSATION

At this point, you may be wondering what has led sociobiologists to redefine rape in such bizarre ways. The answer is found in their particular Weltanschauung. Sociobiologists want to understand behavior primarily in terms of its ultimate causation. They tend to view any existing, genetically influenced behavior as the result of centuries of active natural selection, and from their point of view, any such behavior which has stood the test of natural selection must be adaptive. They then attempt to determine the function of such behaviors through the use of inspection, induction, and/or the creation of plausible explanations (Fedigan, 1982).

This is the approach which sociobiologists have taken in their hypotheses about rape behavior. The implicit assumption is that since rape is such a widespread behavior among men, it must be adaptive — or at the very least, it must have been adaptive in the recent past (See Thornhill and Thornhill, 1983). Adaptive behaviors, by definition, increase the inclusive fitness of animals which use them. In other words, animals possessing adaptive behavioral traits ultimately leave more offspring and descendants than animals that do not have these traits. The concept of inclusive fitness means that not only the animal's direct descendants (i.e., its own offspring), but also its indirect descendants (i.e., the offspring of its parents, siblings and other relatives) will be considered. Using this as a starting point, sociobiologists have tried to explain how rape might increase an individual's inclusive fitness. Two basic hypotheses have been proposed (Thornhill and Thornhill, 1983). The first is that rape is a facultative behavior which is employed by those males who are unable to compete for the resources and status necessary to attract the mates they desire and to reproduce successfully (Alexander, 1978; Thornhill, 1980; Thornhill and Thornhill, 1983). The second hypothesis is that rape is just one of three alternate mating strategies (honest courtship, seduction-deception, and rape) which all males possess (Shields and Shields, 1983). According to this hypothesis, all males are potential rapists. The probability that a particular male will rape depends on his particular circumstances and the probability that rape will result in additional offspring versus the costs of the behavior, including the probability of punishment and its probable severity. The basic premise under both hypotheses is the same: males who rape leave more descendants than equivalent males living under the same conditions who do not rape.

Restrictive definitions of rape, such as that used by Thornhill and Thornhill (1983), arise out the sociobiologists' wish to understand rape primarily in terms of its ultimate causation. Such restrictive definitions of rape seem to me to be artificial, based on circular reasoning and unlikely to offer any significant breakthroughs in our understanding of rape behavior. The term rape is restricted to include only those behaviors which one could logically argue would tend to result in the production of more offspring by the rapist. Thus, rape is adaptive because sociobiologists have limited it by definition to only those behaviors which could easily be argued to be adaptive. Other behaviors, including homosexual rape, rape of women past childbearing or children too young to conceive, incest, forced sexual acts other than vaginal intercourse and rape/murders, which cannot increase a man's inclusive fitness are excluded from consideration. While such a restrictive definition of rape makes it easier for sociobiologists to design persuasive arguments describing how rape behavior might have evolved in animal and human populations, it ignores the reality that all these other categories of rape behavior occur with some frequency in human populations. In fact, the incidence of such rapes is clearly higher than the incidence of rape as defined by the Thornhills (see discussion beginning on p. 29). As long as sociobiologists limit their definition of rape to those cases which might result in pregnancy, the explanatory power of their work will also be limited. The exclusion of behaviors which do not raise the inclusive fitness of the rapist from the category of rape appears to be an artificial division based on theoretical constraints rather than consideration of any characteristics of the behaviors in question.

The theoretical orientation of some sociobiologists also leads them to redefine rape in another way — to describe sexual acts which are not resisted by females as rape. The tendency to describe or interpret particular behavior patterns as rape without documenting evidence of resistance on the part of the presumed victim appears to stem, at least in part, from a somewhat sexist view of animal behavior. A brief theoretical digression is necessary here to illustrate why this might be the case. Sociobiologists are primarily interested in determining how different patterns of social behavior evolved. They are therefore very interested in how different patterns of behavior might affect an animal's reproduction and inclusive fitness. Reproduction requires time, energy, and resources and most writers stress that males and females apportion their reproductive efforts in very different ways (see Halliday, 1980; Trivers, 1972; Wilson, 1975 for further discussion). Sociobiological thinking about such matters is generally couched in terms of economic metaphors, such as costs, benefits and investment strategies, the idea being that natural selection will favor animals that minimize their reproductive costs while maximizing reproduction. According to sociobiological theory, the reproductive strategies of males and females are generally in conflict, because each sex is expected to try to bear the minimal cost necessary to produce each offspring. From this point of view, the optimal strategy is to leave the other parent "holding the baby" and to move on to produce additional offspring with other partners. Such a strategy is seen as being particularly attractive for males, since their seemingly almost limitless production of sperm could theoretically allow them to sire innumerable offspring with a succession of females over their lifetimes. The lifetime reproductive success of females using this strategy is still limited by the finite production of eggs, and in many species by the necessary provision of some maternal care to each offspring.

It is generally argued that females make a greater initial investment in the production of any one offspring because they produce larger gametes than males. In many species, this initial imbalance in reproductive effort between the sexes is further exaggerated by additional parental efforts on the part of females. The most extreme case is found among mammals. Female mammals retain their eggs in the reproductive system following fertilization, providing a safe environment and nourishment for the early development of their young. Following birth, they continue to provide high quality nourishment in the form of milk. Because male mammals lack such specializations for parental care, any contributions to parental care during gestation and lactation tend to be indirect. Males therefore have greater opportunity to abandon a given reproductive effort, forcing the entire burden of parental care onto their mates. Although males do contribute significant amounts of parental care in some species, particularly among birds and fishes, the generalization is usually made that males contribute less parental care than females, and that males can achieve greater reproductive fitness by mating with several females than by limiting their reproductive efforts to one mate.

Because of this inequity in reproductive effort, it is argued that females should be more selective than males in choosing a mate. By far the majority of articles and books dealing with mating strategies stress that because females invest more time and energy in the production of offspring, they should concentrate on obtaining a limited number of high quality matings to maximize their reproductive success. Males, on the other hand, should try to maximize the number of matings they obtain, with quality of the mate being a less important factor. According to this line of reasoning, if a male mates with an unfit female he does not lose very much because all he has invested is sperm. But a female who mates with an unfit male stands to lose a lot because an unsuccessful attempt at reproduction seriously limits her ability to make another attempt. In an extreme case, a female primate that mated with an unfit male might invest years of her life attempting to rear the unfit offspring of that mating to independence. If that offspring dies without leaving offspring itself, she has, in reproductive terms, wasted a great deal of time and "missed" many opportunities to produce additional offspring, thus lowering her fitness. According to this line of thinking, a male primate which made the same poor choice of a mate would only have wasted a negligible amount of sperm and the time it took to approach the female and mate. Not being tied down by the burden of pregnancy and parental care, he can move on to mate again in short order. The available data do seem to bear out the contention that females are more discriminating in their choice of mates than males. For example, male birds of various species have been observed copulating with dead conspecifics, and simple models can easily be used to elicit male copulatory behavior (see Marler and Hamilton, 1966). Similarly, male frogs and toads are noted for their ardor and lack of discriminating during the breeding season. They are apt to clasp anything approximately the size of a female, particularly if it moves, including other males, salamanders, fish, the handle of a net or the finger of an unwary researcher (Halliday, 1980). Females are much more selective in their choice of a mate, and are much more likely to choose a live animal of the appropriate sex and species.

In the case of monogamous animals, sociobiological theorists have taken this reasoning one step further. In such species, males usually contribute substantially to their offsprings' welfare, whether in terms of providing and defending a nest site, providing food, defending the young from predators, socialization, etc. Sociobiologists have suggested that "monogamous" males should try to sneak copulations with additional females, but at the same time try to prevent other males from copulating with their mates (Trivers, 1972). The idea here is that mating with additional females does not take much time or effort on the part of the male, yet it could result in additional offspring which would increase his reproductive success. Sociobiologists argue that the costs of mating are so low for a male, that he should mate at every opportunity on the small chance that it will increase his reproductive success, as long as such secondary matings do not significantly interfere with his aiding his first mate and their offspring. On the other hand, from an evolutionary point of view, it is obviously not in a male's best interest to raise the young of another male. He should therefore guard his mate zealously while she is fertile, to maximize the probability that the offspring he devotes his time and energy to raising are his own.

A number of animal studies have been published in the past ten years purporting to show that males do in fact guard their mates when they are fertile, while at the same time taking advantage of opportunities for extra-pair copulations (e.g., Barash, 1976; Beecher and Beecher, 1979; Hoogland and Sherman, 1976; McKinney and Stolen, 1982; Power and Doner, 1980; Weatherhead and Robertson, 1979). This is a very interesting idea, but one that needs further work. Many studies to date were not properly designed. For example, two studies which are often cited as evidence for mate guarding during the female's fertile period (Barash, 1976; Weatherhead and Robertson, 1979) neglected to control for habituation to repeated presentations of the same models across the breeding season, and this flaw in experimental design seriously undermines their conclusions. In other studies, post hoc interpretations of guarding behavior, though persuasive on one level, could also be replaced by equally persuasive post hoc interpretations. For example, Beecher and Beecher (1979) found that male cliff swallows zealously accompanied their mates every time they left the nest at the time females began to lay and did not chase other females at this time. They interpreted this as mate-guarding during the period of a female's peak fertility when the clutch was being laid. This behavior could be interpreted equally well by a cooperative nestbuilding-courtship hypothesis. Optimal timing of reproduction in this species may require cooperative nestbuilding by males and females. A male might have to devote all his reproductive efforts at this time to nestbuilding with his mate so that the nest is ready to hold the clutch by the time the female is ready to lay. If the nest is not ready, the entire clutch might be lost. Male-female interactions during this period probably play an important role in facilitating ovulation in this species. Thus, a male's nestbuilding with a female and following her from the nest might also be important in stimulating the hormonal changes leading to ovulation and female readiness to incubate.

For females, it is generally assumed that the costs of extra-pair copulations outweigh any possible benefits (see Butler, 1982; Howard, 1978; McKinney, et al., 1983). Very few writers even mention the possibility that females might benefit from mating with more than one male. When a female which is described as paired with one male mates with a second male, the copulation is often described as rape, even though no evidence of resistance on her part is given (Beecher and Beecher, 1979; Butler, 1982; Hoogland and Sherman, 1976; McKinney et al., 1983; Mineau and Cooke, 1979). In such cases, it appears that the classification of extra-pair copulations by females as rape is based on the common assumption, which is somewhat sexist in nature, that one male should be sufficient to satisfy all the reproductive needs of any female — though it is obvious that sociobiologists do not believe the opposite to be true. Such cases give the appearances of applying the sexual double standard to animal behavior. In these cases researchers appear to be interpreting these matings from the viewpoint of the paired male, who evolutionarily stands to lose the most from such sexual interactions, since he might help to raise another male's offspring. They appear to take the classical view of rape as defined under English common law as violation of a mated male's right to exclusive sexual access. No evidence is given that the females were not willing participants in extra-pair matings. The fact that some researchers state that perhaps females may actually welcome some rape attempts (Mineau and Cooke, 1979; McKinney, Derrickson, and Mineau,

1983) points out the difficulty they have in acknowledging that females may be sexually active and willing to engage in extra-pair copulations. Instead, they classify them as male-motivated behavior forced on females, but one which females may not resist. But if females do not resist the males' advances, why call it rape?

There are data from a variety of species generally classed as monogamous that females regularly engage in extra-pair copulations. For example, one study used electrophoresis to investigate paternity in deermice, one of the few rodent species previously described as monogamous (Birdsall and Nash, 1973). The researchers found that 30% of the litters investigated were sired by more than one father. A study of redwinged blackbirds found that when territorial males were vasectomized, their mates still laid fertile eggs if the males on surrounding territories had not also been sterilized (Bray, Kennelly, and Guarino, 1975). This is particularly striking since male redwings are extremely aggressive and do not engage in parental care, at least not early in the breeding season. They spend most of their time guarding their territories and watching over their mates, yet they were unable to prevent successful copulation with neighboring males. Since these studies examined reproductive outcome rather than reproductive behavior, it is impossible to determine whether the extra-pair copulations were forced on the females or if the females were willing participants in such copulations and perhaps even actively solicited them. My own observations of the mating behavior of zebra finches, another supposedly monogamous species, lead me to believe that females may engage in extra-pair copulations much more frequently than is commonly believed. Extra-pair copulations have also been observed in a number of other avian species (see Hoogland and Sherman, 1976).

On an evolutionary level, extra-pair copulations may be very much to a female's advantage. While females are more selective than males in their choice of mates, it is doubtful that females of any species possess the ability to choose the best possible mate from the pool of males available at a given point in time. Given that female choice is bound to be somewhat inaccurate, it is probably to a female's advantage to "hedge her bets" and copulate with several males. This will also protect her from the serious consequences of mating with an infertile male. Most biologists tend to disregard this possibility, equating numbers of male sperm with viability and fertility. However, infertile matings (which can be caused by incompatibility of sperm and eggs as well as pure lack of viability) is a clear danger which females should be selected to avoid. And it may be a more pervasive problem than is commonly thought. We do not have the data which would allow us to determine the frequency of infertility in male animals in their natural habitat. The best data available are for human populations, and they suggest that infertility is common among males trying to reproduce. For example, 20% of American couples suffer from infertility, being unable to conceive a child in one year of uncontracepted intercourse (Mazor, 1979). In at least 50% of these couples (i.e., 10% of American couples), infertility of the man is involved.

It has been argued, and I think rightfully so, that the sociobiological analysis of male-female interactions and reproduction is flawed on several levels. Marshall Sahlins succinctly summarizes a central problem of much sociobiological thinking in stating, "What is inscribed in the theory of sociobiology is the entrenched ideology of Western society: the assurance of its naturalness, and the claim of its inevitability." (Sahlins, 1976, p. 101) Sociobiologists have taken Western economic theory and used it to interpret animal behavior. This is not new, Marx pointed out Darwin's application of capitalistic ideas to the animal world in the latter's theory of natural selection (Sahlins, 1976). But the end product of some sociobiologists' application of economic theory to animal behavior is a theoretical, evolutionary justification of Western society's sexual status quo including the sexual double standard, the greater involvement of females in parental care, and, of particular interest from the point of view of this chapter, males' propensity to rape. But this endpoint was reached because of various assumptions which were made along the way. As Fedigan (1982) points out, the outcome of the sociobiological analysis of male versus female reproductive effort would turn out rather differently if the facts were viewed from a slightly different angle. First, sociobiologists usually argue that from the beginning females make the larger investment in any one offspring because their gametic contribution, the egg, is larger than the male's sperm. Although only one sperm fertilizes a given egg, males invest more than one sperm in a given mating attempt. In fact, they usually invest untold millions. One ejaculation usually releases millions of sperm, and in many species, multiple ejaculations are involved in each mating attempt. In many species of mammals, for example, multiple copulations are essential to insure fertilization of a female's eggs and to stimulate her endocrine system so that the fertilized eggs can implant in the uterus

(Leshner, 1978). One study of fish demonstrated an almost linear decrease in male fertility as mating frequency increased (Nakatsuru and Kramer, 1982), suggesting that there are physiological constraints on male mating efforts. This study also found that females preferred to mate with males that had not recently mated. Second, males' relative lack of discrimination in mating partners must also involve some cost. When talking of the low cost of indiscriminate mating in males, what is usually envisioned is a male happening upon a female, copulating quickly, and then continuing on his merry way. Although this occurs in some species, researchers tend to ignore all the species in which prolonged and/or repeated copulation is necessary to ensure both fertilization of the eggs and their continued development. The amount of time a male must invest in copulation in such species is not trivial. Even in species in which males normally mate with a succession of females, they often consort with each female for several days to a week or more, copulating with great frequency. Consorting indiscriminately could quickly lower a male's reproductive success. A specific example of the costs of indiscriminant mating is found in frogs. A male frog that clasps a salamander rather than a female frog will waste a considerable amount of time attempting to mate with the salamander because the latter cannot give the release croak which a male frog or an unreceptive female utters when clasped by an over-ardent male to secure her release. Under these circumstances, male frogs have been observed to spend entire nights attempting to mate with salamanders, thus missing any chance to actually reproduce. Third, in comparing male and female reproductive efforts, sociobiologists do not take into account the time and energy males spend to reach the point of mating. Although actual copulation may require relatively little time and effort, males have usually invested a great deal of time and effort in obtaining and defending resources to attract females or in competing with other males to gain access to females before they can ever obtain a chance to mate. Males must often compete to obtain and maintain territories or to gain access to female groups. They must not only advertise their presence to females, but often are required to provision a female and/or build her a nest before she will copulate. Many males lose their lives as a direct result of intermale competition or because their advertising displays which evolved to attract females also attract predators (Halliday, 1980). But because males incur these high costs prior to mating, they are usually not compared to postmating costs incurred by females in comparing the relative reproductive efforts of males and females (Fedigan, 1982). Both males and females appear to invest large amounts of time and effort in reproduction, but it is impossible to realistically compare their relative investments.

Even if one ignores these difficulties, there are particular problems in applying this type of sociobiological thinking to human behavior. Many sociobiologists believe that the behavior of people, like that of other animals, has been selected to maximize the individual's reproductive success (Alexander, 1975). In fact, this line of reasoning provides the basis for their theories about the evolution of rape behavior. This does not mean that they think that people are conscious of such selection or feel a conscious need to maximize reproduction, just that over thousands of years, selection will have favored behavior patterns which lead to increased reproductive success and/or inclusive fitness. However, there is a wealth of anthropological evidence, usually ignored by sociobiologists, indicating that contrary to evolutionary theory, people in a variety of cultures are behaving in ways which must detract from their reproductive success and/or inclusive fitness. First, it is obvious that most human populations engage in some form of contraceptive behavior and/or population control, and thus lower their reproductive potential. Arguments can be made that although contraception lowers birth rates, it actually increases the number of surviving offspring. Thus, reproductive success could actually be increased by contraception since reproductive success is determined by surviving offspring, not by fertility. For societies employing contraception primarily as a means of spacing pregnancies several years apart, this argument makes logical sense, though it still needs to be empirically tested. In these cultures, parents may actually raise more children to adulthood by spacing pregnancies and concentrating all their resources on one dependent infant at a time. This line of reasoning has been disputed, however (Livingstone, 1980). But in many cultures, contraception is used to severely limit individuals' reproductive potential. In many industrialized societies, birth rates are now hovering around two children per couple, clearly not a case of reproductive maximization. Evolutionary explanations of this phenomenon are made even more difficult by the fact that birth rates are often negatively correlated with economic status. In other words, those individuals possessing the most economic resources and best able to meet the economic demands of a large family are the least likely individuals to actually have a large family (Livingstone, 1980).

Second, people engage in many other behaviors which demonstrably reduce their reproductive success and/or inclusive fitness. Sociobiologists assume that social organization in humans, like that of other animals, is based on a kin selection model with individuals showing differential behavior towards relatives and nonrelatives. Behavior toward relatives is also expected to be differential, taking into account the degree of relatedness. Sociobiologists expect people to be quite precise in molding their behavior to reflect the precise degree of relatedness. Wilson, for example speaks of the human mind being "sophisticated in the intuitive calculus of blood ties and proportionate altruism." (Wilson, 1975, p. 119–120) But, as Sahlins (1976) points out, there is often very little relationship between biological kinship as calculated by the sociobiologist and socially derived kinship as calculated and acted on by human populations. Sahlins states (p. 26) ". . . there is not a single system of marriage, postmarital residence, family organization, interpersonal kinship, or common descent in human societies that does not set up a different calculus of relationship and social action than is indicated by the principles of kin selection." He goes on to support this assertion with specific examples and extensive coefficients of relationship modeling for a variety of kinship arrangements, arguing quite convincingly that the societal kinship classifications on which social relationships and interactions are based rarely coincide with actual biological kinship relations. For example, in many different cultures men commit the cardinal sin (by sociobiological standards) of raising other men's children as their own. It may happen as a result of the Napoleonic code which is in effect in so many societies. This means that the husband of the mother is regarded as the father of the child, even when such a biological relationship clearly cannot exist. For example, among the Trobrianders, men returning to their families after an absence of a year or more were quite pleased to discover that their wives had had another child in their absence, and such cases were given as evidence that sexual intercourse had nothing to do with conception, since a wife could conceive without having intercourse with her husband, the baby's father (Malinowski, 1929). But probably the most widespread and difficult behavior for sociobiology to explain is adoption, since adoptive parents clearly realize that they are accepting the responsibility of raising a child which is not theirs. Perhaps the most obvious violation of the principles of kin selection was traditional adoption practices in Tahiti. Traditional Tahitians did not adopt children at random, but favored the practice of adopting the child or the nearest kinsman of an enemy one had slain in war. This in itself flies in the face of the principles of kin selection, but beyond this, there was a very high probability that the adopting parents had slain one or more of their own children at birth. In Tahiti, the practice of infanticide was so common, that one highly qualified researcher of Tahitian society concluded that there was hardly a 'married' woman alive who had not lost at least one child through infanticide (Sahlins, 1976). Thus, Tahitian couples would often kill one or more of their own children only to later replace them with unrelated adopted children who had all the rights of their natural children. Presumably the practice of infanticide in this culture has decreased, but the practice of adoption is still widespread. Overall, approximately 25% of all children are adopted, and in some rural villages the percentage of homes containing adopted children runs as high as 38%.

These are just a few of the simplest examples indicating how human behavior patterns often are at odds with sociobiological theorizing about maximization of reproduction. Additional anthropological examples may be found in Sahlins' fascinating extended critique of the application of sociobiological models to human behavior (1976) and in articles by Leacock (1980), Livingstone (1980), and Silverberg (1980). Gould (1980) discusses another problem often ignored by sociobiologists, the relative contributions of cultural evolution versus those of natural selection to the development and stabilization of patterns of human behavior. In presenting evidence against maximization of reproduction and kin selection in human populations, the data presented by these authors calls into question current sociobiological theories about the evolution of rape behavior in human populations, since these theories are based on the basic premise that humans have been selected to maximize reproduction and/or inclusive fitness and that rape behavior is merely one strategy to achieve these ends. Several counterarguments to Sahlins' critique are found in Chagnon and Irons (1979). Perhaps the most credible of these is best presented by Kurland who argues that if one ignores kinship classifications entirely and examines just which persons an individual interacts with, one finds evidence that individuals do indeed interact with their closer biological kin more frequently than other people. This is a reasonable counterargument to Sahlins, but clearly more data are needed to evaluate it, and it does not address all of the issues which Sahlins raises.

DOES RAPE INCREASE MALE FITNESS?

Sociobiologists who have written about the phenomenon posit that rape behavior exists because males who rape leave more offspring and descendants than do males living under similar circumstances who do not rape. This hypothesis is basically untestable under natural conditions. Accurate determination of paternity in wild populations presents serious difficulties. Even if paternity could be accurately established, there would still be the problem of determining males' lifetime reproductive success and inclusive fitness. Not to mention the fact that one would have to know every copulation a male engaged in and which were forced and which were not. It is possible that this hypothesis could be tested in the lab, using a species like *Drosophila* which has a relatively short generation time, but one would have to dedicate an extraordinary amount of time to test this hypothesis, and the applicability of such data to natural populations would always be in question.

In point of fact, there are no data indicating that the various behaviors which sociobiologists have described as rape in various animal species actually result in fertilization of eggs, let alone in an increase in lifetime reproductive success. For example, despite the frequency of behavior described as rape in various avian species, there is no evidence that such behavior has ever resulted in the fertilization of eggs in wild populations (McKinney, et al., 1983). It is not even clear if a male can force cloacal contact with an unwilling female (Mineau and Cooke, 1979). Studies employing models noted that semen was always (Weatherhead and Robertson, 1980), sometimes (Hoogland and Sherman, 1976) or never (Butler, 1982) deposited on models in the course of copulation attempts, and Butler stated that he never witnessed anything resembling a successful forced copulation directed toward a live bird although males regularly mounted models. In the snow goose, Mineau and Cooke (1979) found that "rape attempts" (here defined as a male copulatory attempt with a female other than his mate which was not preceded by the usual precopulatory displays) were independent of the females' fertility, such that the great majority of attempts were directed toward females which were clearly nonfertile. Another study (Power and Doner, 1980) found that males attempted to mount live male decoys significantly more often than female decoys — clearly a nonadaptive strategy. In guppies, Farr (1980) found that males directed rape attempts (here defined as a copulation attempt not preceded by precopulatory displays — no evidence of resistance by females is noted) primarily towards gravid females. Farr cited studies showing that these attempts rarely result in sperm transfer, and that when sperm transfer occurred, it was minimal. In orangutans, the only primate species in which forced copulation has been described, males, usually adolescents, occasionally attempt forced copulations with nonestrous females (Galdikas, 1979; MacKinnon, 1974, 1979). This strongly suggests that such copulations never result in fertilization, since ovulation in females is strongly associated with the occurrence of estrus. Beyond this, MacKinnon goes on to state that it is very unlikely that male orangutans can achieve intromission unless the female cooperates, and cooperation is highly unlikely unless the female is in estrus. Data from other species indicate that males appear to attempt copulations primarily when females are known to be fertile (Beecher and Beecher, 1979; Butler, 1982; Hoogland and Sherman, 1976; Remember that no evidence of resistance by females was presented in these studies). The available data (McKinney, et al., 1983) do not allow any clear decision as to whether dabbling ducks which are so prone to forced copulations are more likely to direct their forced copulation attempts toward fertile females. It is clear that males often direct attempts at infertile females, either before the start of the breeding season or once females have begun to incubate. The relative proportion of attempts directed toward fertile and infertile females remains unclear because most studies defined fertility so broadly (e.g., during the breeding season females were considered fertile, even though females sitting on completed clutches would not be). Further, one must always keep in mind, that even if it is demonstrated at some later time that forced copulations result in fertilization, this does not assure the male increased fitness. It must be shown that the resulting offspring survive and go on to reproduce themselves, and that males which engage in forced copulations leave more descendants than those males who do not.

Determining whether rape in humans increases a man's fitness is a similarly daunting problem. However, one can logically argue that it seems unlikely that rape would significantly enhance reproductive success or inclusive fitness. The probability that a single episode of rape in humans will result in pregnancy appears to be very low. In the absence of good data on the frequency with which rape results in pregnancy, one can make some simple calculations based on the statistics available for the United States. Of course, these calculations are limited by the information available. Most sources agree that rape is the most underreported violent crime in the United States and that only about 20% of all rapes are reported to the police (Hyde, 1982; Masters, Johnson, and Kolodny, 1982; Nass, Libby, and Fisher, 1981). The available statistics are of course based on reported rapes, and one cannot know how the details of reported rapes differ from those that are not reported. Given these caveats, the probability that attempted sexual assaults will result in pregnancy is calculated in Table 1. First of all, studies show that in 75% of attempted sexual assaults, the woman manages to successfully resist the attacker (Masters, et al., 1982). Second, one out of every five hundred rape victims is killed by the rapist (Brownmiller, 1975). Third, over 50% of reported sexual assaults involve behaviors other than vaginal intercourse (Hyde, 1982), the most frequent behaviors being anal intercourse or fellatio, though insertion of objects into the vagina is also common (DeLora, Warren and Ellison, 1981). Fourth, rapists suffer from very high levels of sexual dysfunction. It is now generally recognized that the requirement that traces of semen be found on/in the victim to corroborate her claim of rape is unfair, because such a large proportion of rapists

Table 1. Estimated number of pregnancies resulting from 1000 attempted sexual assaults in the United States.

	Number of cases remaining
Attempted sexual assaults	1000
75% of victims fend off attempted assault	250
1 victim per 500 is killed by the rapist	249.5
50% of assaults involve acts other than vaginal intercourse	125
40% of rapists experience sexual dysfunction	50
14.6% of victims probably too young or old to bear children	42.7
82% of victims raped during infertile portion of menstrual cycle	6.8
70% probability that intercourse on most fertile day of cycle will not result in pregnancy	2.0
20% of all pregnancies result in spontaneous abortions	1.6

suffer from ejaculatory difficulty. The precise proportion of rapists suffering from sexual dysfunction varies from study to study, the proportion ranging from 33% to 40% to as high as 58%, but in all studies is higher than the rate of dysfunction found in the general population (Masters, et al., 1982; Nass, et al., 1981). Problems included in this category such as difficulty initiating and maintaining erection, inability to ejaculate, and premature ejaculation before intromission can be achieved, all make it highly unlikely that fertilization could occur. Fifth, although the majority of rape attempts are directed toward women of childbearing age, women of all ages have been raped, from infants to women in their eighties and nineties. Most data on the incidence of rape categorize rape victims according to very broad age categories, and none, as far as I am aware, breaks the data down according to the reproductive status of the victim. Using the data presented by Shields and Shields (1983) on the age distribution of reported rape victims, another 7.7% of rapes can be classed as unlikely to result in pregnancy, since the victims involved were either under the age of 10 or above the age of 50. Clearly, a greater proportion of rapes involve victims who are either incapable or unlikely to be able to carry a pregnancy to term. The average age of menarche in the United States is 12.8 years for whites and 12.5 years for blacks (Masters, et al., 1982), and ovulation does not usually occur in the first two years after menarche (Apter, Viinikka, and Vihko, 1978). Beyond that, the maturing reproductive system is usually not capable of carrying a pregnancy to term for at least another year following the initiation of ovulation (Frisch, 1980). At the other end of the reproductive spectrum, approximately 50% of women undergo menopause before the age of 50 (Stewart, Guest, Stewart, and Hatcher, 1979), and menopause is preceded by a six or seven year period of declining fertility (Frisch, 1980). So clearly, there are many women unable to bear children who would be included in the remaining calculations using the Shields' data. If one uses the data presented in Thornhill and Thornhill (1983) and excludes when possible all data from girls under the age of 12 and women over 45, who are unlikely to be fertile, and 50% of the data from girls between the ages of 12–15 who have a significantly lower fertility than adults, this would exclude approximately 15% of rape victims on grounds of infertility. The data presented from MacDonald (1971) were excluded from this calculation because they contain several empty age categories and have a very unusual age distribution. Sixth, even among women who are capable of bearing a child, most are raped during infertile portions of the menstrual cycle. There is absolutely no evidence that men are more likely to rape women at the time of ovulation than at any other point in the menstrual cycle or that sexual intercourse can induce ovulation. Using a menstrual cycle of 28 days which probably underestimates average cycle length, and a liberal interpretation of sperm and egg viability in a woman's reproductive tract, a woman is fertile only during about 16% of the cycle (Stewart, et al., 1979). Seventh, the chance that a woman will become pregnant from one act of intercourse, even on the most fertile day of her cycle, is rather low — about 30% (Stewart, et al., 1979). This percentage may be slightly higher if an individual is raped several times. Finally, a significant portion of all pregnancies end in spontaneous abortions, usually between the fourth and twelfth weeks of pregnancy (Hyde, 1982; Stewart, et al. 1979). Estimates of the proportion of pregnancies terminated by spontaneous abortion vary tremendously, primarily because spontaneous abortions during the first two months of pregnancy are rarely recognized as such. The incidence of spontaneous abortion has been estimated to be somewhere between 15–50% of all pregnancies. Using a spontaneous abortion rate of 20%, this means that out of 1000 attempted sexual assaults, probably less than two women will become pregnant and be able to carry the baby to term if they wanted to. Although I have tried to be somewhat conservative in my calculations and not use the most extreme statistics available to make my point, this is a low success rate from any point of view.

Even if a child is conceived as a result of rape, chances that the mother will rear it to adulthood seem slim. She may have been seriously injured by the attack or contracted a venereal disease which would adversely affect the continuation of the pregnancy and/or the health of the child. Adolescent girls who are the favored targets of rapists (Shields and Shields, 1983) have not matured sufficiently to withstand the rigors of pregnancy, birth and motherhood. Pregnancy in adolescents involves greater risks of maternal and offspring mortality and morbidity, including a wide range of serious birth defects (Austen and Short, 1980). In our culture, adolescents are also more likely to abuse their children than are older mothers. In many cultures, including to some extent our own, rape victims are ostracized; in other cultures, they may even be punished along with the rapist (Brownmiller, 1975). Alienated from family and friends, rape victims often have very little in the way of resources to support themselves, let alone a child. Many attempt abortion, and if that fails, infanticide (Brownmiller, 1975). Others, as was evident in Bangladesh, find the circumstances so daunting that they choose suicide. According to a recent survey of rape victims in the United States, 16% had nervous breakdowns and 19% attempted suicide as a result of being raped (Stark, 1985). Clearly, the odds do not favor the successful rearing of a child conceived under such circumstances. Sociobiologists admit that the probability that rape will result in conception is low (see Shields and Shields, 1983; Thornhill and Thornhill, 1983), but maintain that even the slightest increase in the reproductive success of rapists would tend to maintain such behavior in human populations. Until forced copulation is demonstrated to increase the reproductive success and/or inclusive fitness of males which engage in such behavior in some species, I remain skeptical of this argument.

There are other reasons for doubting that reproductive success is the underlying motivating factor in human rape. First, in many cases of rape in humans, assault seems to be the important factor, not sex. One study found that 25% of reported rapes involved slapping the victim around, 20% reported beating the victim to the extent that the attack was classified as brutal, and 12% involved choking the victim. Group assaults, which account for 25–40% of reports, tend to be more violent than individual assaults (Offir, 1982). In most cases, the use of force goes beyond that necessary to compel the victim's compliance with the rapist's demands. Objects, such as sticks, bottles and knives are often inserted in the victim's vagina. The breasts and genitals may be mutilated. Among reported rapes, use of a weapon occurs in about 50% of the cases. In 10% of the cases where victim and rapist are strangers, the rape results in a battered victim suffering broken bones, internal injuries and/or knife and gun wounds. If the primary purpose of rape is reproduction, why is injury inflicted on the victim? Clearly such injuries adversely affect the victim's physiological capacity to carry a pregnancy to term and her psychological desire to do so. Secondly, if the primary purpose of the rapist is to sire a child, then the high proportion of group assaults is problematic, since the probability that a particular individual will father a child is lower than if he had raped the woman by himself. Thirdly, 7% of reported rapes and 32% of cases in which children are raped involve relatives who are men (Hyde, 1979; Masters, et al., 1982), and this proportion may very well be higher in rapes which are not reported to the authorities. Such incestuous rapes tend to lower the fitness of the man, as explained by Shields and Shields (1983), and therefore run counter to sociobiological hypotheses about rape behavior. Finally, recent psychological studies have demonstrated that men who rape differ from non-rapists in their sexual arousal (Masters, et al., 1982). Both rapists and non-rapists developed erections while listening to descriptions of mutually consenting individuals engaging in intercourse, but only rapists responded sexually to descriptions of rape. Rapists showed similar levels of arousal to both types of description. These data suggest that the idea that every man is a potential rapist, although theoretically possible ignores psychological characteristics which may predispose men toward or away from rape. Examination of women's descriptions of being raped (Brownmiller, 1975; Masters, et al., 1982; Russell, 1975) indicates that some rapists are only able to function sexually when they have total power over their victims while others can only maintain an erection as long as the victim resists. Certainly, sexual arousal in most men is not contingent on these particular circumstances.

SUMMARY

Some sociobiologists interested in the evolution of human behavior examined various hypotheses on the causation of rape and found them unsatisfactory. Unlike many other theorists, they felt that rape was not a uniquely human behavior, but one which was shown by a wide variety of animals from invertebrates to non-human primates. In particular, they felt that existing hypotheses had ignored factors contributing to the evolution and maintenance of rape behavior in animal and human populations. They examined rape from an evolutionary perspective and suggested that rape occurs because rapists leave more descendants on average than do males in similar circumstances who do not rape. According to their theories, rapists have a reproductive advantage over non-rapists.

In this chapter, I have endeavored to point out various flaws in this line of reasoning. There are problems of definition and semantics. First, applying anthropomorphic terms, such as rape, to non-human animals is objectionable because it is imprecise, sensationalistic and implies a similarity of form, function and proximate causation between human and animal behavior which has not been demonstrated (Estep and Bruce, 1981; Gowaty, 1981). More neutral terms such as forced copulation or resisted mating are preferable.

Second, no matter what one labels the behavior, a particular problem in investigating forced and/or resisted copulations is that it implies that scientists can unequivocally determine when a copulation is forced and when it is not. But protracted resistance is a normal part of female sexual behavior in many species (Estep and Bruce, 1981) and the larger size of males in many sexually dimorphic species often leads observers to think that males are forcing themselves on females when they are not (McKinney, et al., 1983). Third, when sociobiologists use the term rape, their definition is usually different from either common usage (i.e., a sexual act forced on an individual against its will) or the legal or scientific definitions used in other studies (Estep and Bruce, 1981), and this difference in definitions is usually not made explicit. For example, in many studies purporting to demonstrate the existence of rape in animal populations, sociobiologists labeled copulations in which the participants did not engage in precopulatory displays as rape, even though there was no evidence that the females resisted the males' sexual advances. But female resistance, however difficult to evaluate, would seem to be a hallmark of forced copulation. If these studies are reconsidered and copulations are considered forced only when there is evidence of the female's resistance, then one learns that claims that forced copulations are found in a wide variety of species from invertebrates to nonhuman primates do not hold. Forced copulations appear among males of a rather limited number of species. Thus, sociobiologists do not have the broad foundation across phyla they claim. Even when sociobiologists apply the term rape to human behavior, their meaning often diverges from common usage. For example, in discussing the occurrence of rape in human populations, the Thornhills (Thornhill and Thornhill, 1983) use a much more limited definition of rape which excludes many of the behaviors commonly considered to be rape by either common usage or legal definition. Among the sexual behaviors performed against a woman's will but excluded from their definition of rape are incest, fellatio, anal intercourse, vaginal intercourse with girls too young and women too old to bear children and even vaginal intercourse resulting in pregnancy if such rape increases the reproductive fitness of the woman or decreases that of the rapist. Fourth, sociobiologists' tendency to redefine terms in specialized ways results in circular reasoning. For example, the Thornhills' state that rape behavior has evolved because males who rape leave more descendants on average than males who do not rape. They go on to redefine rape, restricting it to include only those classes of sexual assault which could logically be expected to result in the production of more offspring by the rapist. Another example of circular reasoning is found in the assertion (Thornhill and Thornhill, 1983, p. 158), "As might be expected from an evolutionary perspective of the influence of rape on female fitness, resistance by victims seems to be a feature of rape to a greater extent than in certain other crimes." It would seem obvious that women who report that they have been raped will also report that they resisted the assault of the rapist. A rape victim must prove that she resisted the sexual advances of the rapist if she is to legally prove that she was raped. There is no other crime for which the victim is expected to report resistance to prove that the crime occurred. Fifth, sociobiological hypotheses about rape assume that humans have been strongly selected to maximize their reproduction and exhibit kin selection. There is a wealth of anthropological evidence which contradicts these assumptions, although there is also some which supports them. Sixth, sociobiological hypotheses about rape assume that the evolution and maintenance of rape behavior have been favored because males who rape enjoy a reproductive advantage over males who do not. There is absolutely no evidence from either animal or human populations supporting this premise, and given the current state of our expertise, this hypothesis is basically untestable. Finally, sociobiological reasoning about rape contains some rather obvious sexual and cultural biases (Caplan, 1983; Leacock, 1980; Sahlins, 1976). To some extent, biases are to be expected in any scientific hypothesis, because scientific thinking reflects the cultural perspective of its originator. On the other hand, such biases are objectionable because sociobiologists claim to develop general laws of social behavior which they apply in a disinterested fashion to human behavior. But the sociobiological articles reviewed for this chapter suggested that the Western sexual double standard is natural and occurs among animal as well as human populations and that males have evolved a programmed propensity to rape which is universal and probably recalcitrant to reprogramming as a result of individual experience (Shields and Shields, 1983). Thornhill and Thornhill (1983, p. 141) also state that one of the primary results of rape from the victim's perspective is that she is denied "the option of exchanging sexual favors for social position or material gain." In other words, a victim of rape is "damaged goods" and has lost the opportunity of prostituting herself for future gain. In this case, the researchers' biases have prevented them from grasping even the most basic understanding of rape from the victim's perspective. For all the reasons listed above, I think that current sociobiological hypotheses are unlikely to offer any significant breakthroughs in our understanding of the causation and incidence of rape. In reaching this conclusion, I do not intend to criticize all sociobiological thinking. Clearly, only a limited number of sociobiologists have contributed to the literature discussed, and sociobiological theory has made a number of important contributions to the field of behavioral biology. However, sociobiology as a whole is liable to be discredited by hypothesizing of the type described in this chapter — at least with those who judge science by its respect for evidence and rigor of argument.

ACKNOWLEDGEMENTS

I thank Drs. Sarah Lenington, Peter Moller, Robert Sapolsky, and Carol Simon for their comments on earlier drafts of this chapter. I am particularly indebted to Dr. Colin Beer for his discussions of semantic and conceptual issues in science and for his example of clarity and rigor in scientific thought.

REFERENCES

Alexander, R.D. (1975). The search for a general theory of behavior. *Behavioral Science, 20,* 77–100.

Alexander, R.D. (1978). Natural selection and societal laws. In T. Englehardt and D. Callahan (Eds.) *The foundations of ethics and its relationship to science, Vol. 3: Morals, science and society* (pp. 138–182). Hastings-on-Hudson, NY: Hastings Institute.

Apter, D., Viinikka, L., and Vihko, R. (1978). Hormonal pattern of adolescent menstrual cycles. *Journal of Clinical Endocrinology and Metabolism, 47,* 944–954.

Austen, C.R. and Short, R.V. (1980). *Reproduction in mammals, Vol 8: Human sexuality.* New York: Cambridge University Press.

Barash, D.P. (1976). Male response to apparent female adultery in the mountain bluebird: An evolutionary interpretation. *American Naturalist, 110,* 1097–1101.

Barash, D.P. (1977). *Sociobiology and behavior.* New York: Elsevier.

Barlow, G.W. (1967). Social behavior of a South American leaf fish, *Polycentrus schomburgkii,* with an account of recurring pseudofemale behavior. *American Midland Naturalist, 78,* 215–234.

Beach, F.A. (1979). Animal models and psychological inference. In H.A. Katchadourian (Ed.), *Human sexuality, (pp. 98–112)*. Berkeley, CA: University of California Press.

Beecher, M.D. and Beecher, I.M. (1979). Sociobiology of bank swallows: Reproductive strategy of the male. *Science, 205,* 1282–1285.

Beer, C. (1983). Motives and metaphors in considerations of animal nature. In D.W. Pfaff (Ed.), *Ethical questions in brain and behavior: Problems and opportunities,* (pp. 125–140). New York: Springer Verlag.

Birdsall, D.A. and Nash, D. (1973). Occurrence of successful multiple insemination of females in natural populations of deer mice *(Peromyscus maniculatus). Evolution, 27,* 106–110.

Bray, O.E., Kennelly, J.J. and Guarino, J.L. (1975). Fertility of eggs produced on territories of vasectomized red-winged blackbirds. *Wilson Bulletin, 87,* 187–195.

Brownmiller, S. (1975). *Against our will: Men, women and rape.* New York: Simon and Schuster.

Butler, R.W. (1982). Wing fluttering by mud-gathering cliff swallows: Avoidance of "rape" attempts? *Auk, 90,* 758–761.

Caplan, A.L. (1983). Out with the "old" and in with the "new" — The evolution and refinement of sociobiological theory. In D.W. Pfaff (Ed.), *Ethical questions in brain and behavior* (pp. 91–110). New York: Springer Verlag.

Chagnon, N.A. and Irons, W. (Eds., 1979). *Evolutionary biology and human social behavior: An anthropological perspective.* North Scituate, MA: Duxbury Press.

Cox, C.R. and Le Boeuf, B.J. (1977). Female incitation of male competition: A mechanism in sexual selection. *American Naturalist, 111,* 317–335.

DeLora, J.S., Warren, C.A.B., and Ellison, C.R. (1981). *Understanding sexual interaction.* Boston: Houghton Mifflin.

Estep, D.Q. and Bruce, K.E.M. (1981). The concept of rape in non-humans: A critique. *Animal Behaviour, 29,* 1272–1273.

Farr, J.A. (1980). The effects of sexual experience and female receptivity on courtship-rape decisions in male guppies, *Poecilia reticulata. Animal Behaviour, 28,* 1195–1202.

Fedigan, L.M. (1982). *Primate paradigms: Sex roles and social bonds.* Montreal, Canada: Eden Press.

Frisch, R.E. (1980). Fatness, puberty, and fertility. *Natural History, 89(10),* 16–27.

Galdikas, B. (1979). Orangutan adaptation at Tanjung Puting Reserve: Mating and ecology. In: D.A. Hamburg and E.R. McGown (Eds.), *The great apes* (pp. 195–233). Menlo Park, CA: Benjamin/Cummings.

Gould, S.J. (1980). Sociobiology and the theory of natural selection. In G.W. Barlow and J. Silverberg (Eds.), *Sociobiology: Beyond nature/ nurture?* AAAS Selected Symposium 35 (pp. 257–272). Boulder, CO: Westview Press.

Gowaty, P.A. (1980). Sexual terms in sociobiology: Emotionally evocative and paradoxically, jargon. *Animal Behaviour, 30,* 630–631.

Halliday, T. (1980) *Sexual strategy.* Chicago: University of Chicago Press.

Hoogland, J.L. and Sherman, P.W. (1976). Advantages and disadvantages of bank swallow (*Riparia riparia*) coloniality. *Ecological Monographs, 46,* 33–58.

Howard, R.D. (1978). The evolution of mating strategies in bullfrogs, *Rana catesbeiana. Evolution, 32,* 850–871.

Hyde, J.S. (1982). *Understanding human sexuality.* New York: McGraw-Hill.

Keenleyside, M.H.A. (1972). Intraspecific intrusion into nests of spawning longear sunfish (*Pisces: Centrarchidae*). *Copeia, 2,* 272–278.

Kodric-Brown, A. (1977). Reproductive success and the evolution of breeding territories in pupfish (*Cyprinodon*). *Evolution, 31,* 750–766.

Leacock, E. (1980). Social behavior, biology and the double standard. In G.W. Barlow and J. Silverberg (Eds.), *Sociobiology: Beyond nature/nurture?* AAAS Selected Symposium 35 (pp. 465–488). Boulder, CO: Westview Press.

Leshner, A.I. (1978). *An introduction to behavioral endocrinology.* New York: Oxford University Press.

Livingstone, F.B. (1980). Cultural cause and genetic change. In G.W. Barlow and J. Silverberg (Eds.), *Sociobiology: Beyond nature/nurture?* AAAS Selected Symposium 35 (pp. 307–330). Boulder, CO: Westview Press.

MacKinnon, J. (1974). *In search of the red ape.* New York: Holt, Rinehart and Winston.

MacKinnon, J. (1979). Reproductive behavior in wild orangutan populations. In: D.A. Hamburg and E.R. McGown (Eds.), *The great apes* (pp. 257–273). Menlo Park, CA: Benjamin/Cummings.

Malinowski, B. (1929). *The sexual life of savages in north-western Melanesia.* New York: Eugenics Publishing.

Manning, A. (1967). The control of sexual receptivity in female *Drosophila. Animal Behaviour, 15,* 239–250.

Marler, P. and Hamilton III, W.J. (1966). *Mechanisms of animal behavior.* New York: John Wiley and Sons.

Masters, W.H., Johnson, V.E. and Kolodny, R.C. (1982). *Human sexuality.* Boston: Little, Brown and Company.

Mazor, M.D. (1979, May). Barren couples. *Psychology Today,* 101–112.

McKinney, F., Barrett, J., and Derrickson, S.R. (1978). Rape among mallards. *Science, 201,* 281–282.

McKinney, F., Derrickson, S.R., and Mineau, P. (1983). Forced copulation in waterfowl. *Behaviour,* 250–294.

McKinney, F. and Stolen, P. (1982). Extra-pair-bond courtship and forced copulation among captive green-winged teal (*Anas crecca carolinensis*). *Animal Behaviour, 30,* 461–474.

Mineau, P. and Cooke, F. (1979). Rape in the lesser snow goose. *Behaviour,* *70,* 280–291.

Nakatsuru, K. and Kramer, D.L. (1982). Is sperm cheap? Limited male fertility and female choice in the lemon tetra (*Pisces, Characidae*). *Science,* *216,* 753–755.

Nass, G.D., Libby, R.W. and Fisher, M.P. (1981). *Sexual choices.* North Scituate, MA: Wadsworth Health Sciences Division.

Offir, C.W. (1982). *Human sexuality.* New York: Harcourt Brace Jovanovich.

Power, H.W. and Doner, C.G.P. (1980). Experiments in cuckoldry in the mountain bluebird. *American Naturalist, 116,* 689–704.

Russell, D.E.H. (1975). *The politics of rape: The victim's perspective.* New York: Stein and Day.

Sahlins, M. (1976). *The use and abuse of biology.* Ann Arbor, MI: University of Michigan Press.

Shields, W.M. and Shields, L.M. (1983). Forcible rape: An evolutionary perspective. *Ethology and Sociobiology, 4,* 115–136.

Silverberg, J. (1980). Sociobiology, the new synthesis? An anthropologist's perspective — In G.W. Barlow and J. Silverberg (Eds.), *Sociobiology: Beyond nature/nurture?* AAAS Selected Symposium 35 (pp. 25–76). Boulder, CO: Westview Press.

Stark, E. (1985, February). The psychological aftermath. *Psychology Today,* 48.

Stewart, F., Guest, F., Stewart, G., and Hatcher, R. (1979). *My body, my health: The concerned woman's guide to gynecology.* New York: John Wiley and Sons.

Thornhill, R. (1980). Rape in *Panorpa* scorpionflies and a general rape hypothesis. *Animal Behaviour, 28,* 52–59.

Thornhill, R. and Thornhill, N.W. (1983). Human rape: An evolutionary analysis. *Ethology and Sociobiology, 4,* 137–173.

Trivers, R.L. (1972). Parental investment and sexual selection. In B. Campbell (Ed.), *Sexual selection and the descent of man* (pp. 136–179). Chicago: Aldine.

Weatherhead, P.J. and Robertson, R.J. (1980). Sexual recognition and anticuckoldry behavior in savannah sparrows. *Canadian Journal of Zoology, 58,* 991–996.

Wells, K.D. (1977). The social behavior of anuran amphibians. *Animal Behaviour, 25,* 666–693.

Wilson, E.O. (1975). *Sociobiology.* Cambridge, MA: Harvard University Press.

SOCIAL PSYCHOLOGICAL ASPECTS OF RAPE

Florence L. Denmark and Susan B. Friedman
HUNTER COLLEGE, CUNY

A recent gang rape in a New Bedford bar illustrates how social psychological aspects of rape can affect the life of an individual woman, an entire community and a country.

Again the notion of a woman "hanging out" and drinking alone in a bar, has been raised as evidence to try to justify gang rape. We have been hearing old sayings such as "she shouldn't have been there in the first place," or "she really wasn't a nice girl anyway and she got what she deserved."

Some people feel they have the right to ask whether the victim was flirtatious and provocative or why she was in an environment conducive to sexual harassment in the first place. But, what do these questions have to do with justifying rape? Nothing, because nothing can justify rape. Rape is a violent, aggressive crime. No one benefited from the Cable News Network's coverage of this trial. How much care and concern was there for the mind, body and health of the victim? Her name has appeared publicly, and she has been forced to move away from her home to maintain an element of safety and privacy. Isn't it strange that a victim of rape remains a victim even after she has been assaulted? How many people are still saying that "she asked for it" or "she is to blame?"

MYTHS ABOUT RAPE

There is a long list of myths about rape. Defined in common sources such as Roget's College Thesaurus and Webster's Dictionary the word myth refers to "imaginary, make-believe, unverifiable people or things, legend, tradition, phantasy, fiction and falsehood." Myths about rape, *falsehoods* about rape? How and why has such a powerfully real crime been transformed into a tradition of socially and psychologically acceptable behavior? Ironically, these falsehoods about rape have become commonly encouraged in many societies through mythology, the just world phenomenon, misplaced and distorted attribution of responsibility and through mass media, pornography and violence against women. Where and what are the roots that have allowed the encouragement and acceptance of violence against women to begin and become a part of most existing cultures? What purpose can rape have for ever existing?

In a study done at the University of Bombay, India (Kanekar & Kolsawalla, 1980) the issues and surrounding myths about rape victims with regard to their "respectability, attractiveness and provocativeness" were examined. This was done to determine whether or not the rape victim is held responsible for her own rape. If the victim was married she received greater respect in both the U.S.A. and India (Kanekar & Kolsawalla, 1977) than did a woman who was divorced. In addition, the victim was considered either "very good-looking" or "not at all good-looking." Her manner of dress was described as either dressed sexually provocatively or not dressed sexually provocatively. These descriptions were used to measure the victim's attractiveness and provocativeness. Although men credited the rape victim with greater responsibility than did females, and, in turn, women advocated longer prison sentences than did men, one notable result indicated that the victim who was considered provocative was held more accountable than the unprovocative victim by both men and women. Supporting a common rape myth, the provocative, attractive and divorced woman is seen as more *responsible* for being raped than the unattractive, married woman. Psychologically juxtapose this myth with the sexy, handsome man who is advertized as desirable and successful, and we can see the discrimination that is planted against women.

Most social psychological studies (e.g., Kanekar and Kolsawalla, 1980; Malamuth and Check, 1981) have concluded that people, especially men, maintain and believe in a varied assortment of myths about rape. One common myth is that the victim gets what she deserves and the result of this myth is that the victim is blamed. Although the values and beliefs in our society are changing, slowly, we still do live in a patriarchal society. Therefore, blaming the victim serves somehow to justify and support violence against women. Instead of investigating why the victim is so often blamed, what is presented to us are myths, another of which is the idea that women who are targets of sex crimes have a psychological need to become victims (Dullea, 1979). If we accept this falsehood, we accept the myth that the victim not only needs to become victimized / raped / abused, but also that she wants to participate in becoming a victim or that she in fact was not raped at all but needed to make people believe she was (Sheffield, 1984). The myth that the rape victim gets what she deserves creates energy and space for an off-shoot myth, the theme of masochism. Freud's theory invited and encouraged the idea that women have a masochistic tendency for suffering due to the pleasures and pains found in their reproductive and sexual events. If the notion of women possessing masochistic tendencies is accepted as an innate part of their psychological makeup, then she becomes a born victim. Consequently, she is expected to *ask for it*. This myth powerfully serves to ease the severity of the crime and release the rapist of his responsibility. The victim in effect is the seducer and the rapist is fulfilling his natural, biological drives. We again blame the victim and she becomes the guilty person both emotionally and socially.

If we examine the following list of rape myths, it is evident that the myths all point to the victim as if to say, "she asked for it," and, if she asked for it, she is responsible. Relentlessly she is viewed as the seducer and the true offender is condoned.

1) The victim gets what she deserves and the victim is blamed.

2) She gets what she deserves because we live in a just world, and there is a rational reason for everything that happens.

3) In terms of attribution theory, victims are blamed because of certain characteristics such as provocativeness or flirtatiousness. This in turn gives some men the *right* to think they were seduced and to retaliate with rape.

4) Men are taught to be aggressive which in turn may be psychologically and socially linked with success and sexual

behavior. Susan Brownmiller and other feminists have proposed that sexual aggression toward women becomes socially acceptable when the existence of strong, gender-role stereotypes within a society are encouraged (Watson, deBortali-Tregerthan and Frank, 1984).

5) All women want to be raped.

6) When she says no, she means yes.

7) If you are going to be raped, you might as well enjoy it.

8) If a woman can't fight off a rapist, she must really want to be raped.

9) Women provoke rape by the way they dress, their behavior and actions.

10) Only young and attractive women are raped.

11) A woman cannot be raped by her husband, because rape only occurs between strangers.

12) Initially women will resist being raped. However, because of female, masochistic tendencies they will surrender to the rapist and enjoy the assault.

13) All rapists are poor, ethnic minority types (Herman, 1984).

The ongoing acceptance of gender role stereotyping appears to be one of the roots for the continuance and encouragement of a rape culture. The roles men and women are assigned and play in our society are characterized by very specific thoughts and accompanying behavior. "Women are taught to be passive in thought, word, and sexual deed, while men are taught to be aggressive in any and all sexual situations" (Campbell, 1975, p. 20). The woman who is true to herself, her feelings and ideas, and behaves as she chooses runs the risk of being considered unfeminine and pushy. Should her behavior appear to be aggressive, then she may be viewed as wanting to be raped (Campbell, 1975). On the opposite side of this equally mythological picture is the view of man. His masculinity is measured by both sexual and non-sexual aggression, both of which are encouraged and expected if he is to be considered a "real man" (Campbell, 1975). This socialization for both men and women, which includes the instillation of gender role stereotyping, false expectations, and lack of communication, sets the scene for many rape crimes.

In a similar vein, the violent myths about wife battering include:

1) Some women need to be beaten.

2) A good kick in the ass will straighten her out.

3) She needs a punch in the mouth every so often to keep her in line.

4) She must have done something to provoke him (Sheffield, 1984).

There is a tremendous similarity between these myths and the ones that exist about rape. Consistently what is being said in all these myths is that the victim is asking for it. If these myths are repetitively reinforced, then it will not be surprising that the incidence of violence against women continues to grow.

In 1980 Martha Burt conducted a study, the purpose of which was to see if there was a correlation between people's attitudes about romantic and sexual behavior and their attitudes about rape and sexual assault. Burt measured the participants' attitudes about gender role stereotyping, distrust of the other sex and interpersonal violence by having them respond to such items as:

1) There is something wrong with a woman who doesn't want to marry and raise a family.

2) In a dating relationship a woman is largely out to take advantage of a man.

3) A man is never justified in hitting his wife.

The participants' responses to these items were then correlated with agreement statements that were indicative of rape myths, such as "in the majority of rapes the victim is promiscuous or has a bad reputation." Burt's study indicated that people who had strong stereotypical attitudes about the sexes, believed in adversarial relationships between men and women, and assented to interpersonal violence were more likely to believe in rape myths. However, younger and better educated participants were less likely to hold strong beliefs about gender role stereotyping and rape myths.

In a study conducted by Malamuth, Haber and Feshbach (1980) male and female college students were asked: if a woman was raped and no one knew about it, would she enjoy the experience? The men estimated 32 percent of these women would enjoy it compared to 27 percent of the women who said they would. Women were then confronted with a slight variation of the original question. They were asked: personally would they enjoy being raped if no one knew about it? Ninety-eight percent said they would not.

It has been suggested that women, in the roles of wife and mother, are responsible for the occurrence of rape. Palm and Abrahamsen (1954) conducted a study of wives of rapists. These women did not fulfill the traditional, feminine, passive sex-roles and in addition, they were sexually unreceptive to their husbands. The study implies that as a result of the wife's extended sexual unresponsiveness her husband becomes sexually frustrated and is driven to rape. The blame is shifted away from the rapist to the rapist's innocent wife.

A variation of blaming the victim is also seen in the following study (McCaldon, 1967). The mother is held accountable for her son's behavior. McCaldon suggested that as a child, if a son's needs are frustrated, the mother is responsible for the child's discomfort. The son learns to vent his anger at his mother and later in life, women become the objects of his pent-up aggression. One might question why there is an exclusion of the father and his responsibility for fulfilling the child's needs. By including the father, the responsibility for the son would fall on both the father and the mother, and would equally distribute possible blame and responsibility between both parents. In the last two studies, the woman is placed in a no-win position. Not only is she responsible for her own actions, but she is also responsible for the man's actions, his interpretations of her actions and in essence, all the things that might give him an excuse to lose control (Medea and Thompson, 1974). The father/ husband/son is released from his responsibility yet the mother/ wife/daughter is held accountable.

JUST WORLD PHENOMENON

If we examine the distribution of blame based on these myths, we see that blame of the victim is based on such characteristics as the woman's provocativeness, flirtatiousness and/or her presupposed, innate need and desire to be raped. Yet in reality, it is this list of myths that puts her in a double-bind position. Women are taught to be passive, weak and dependent and to look to a man for protection. Throughout their childhood, women are taught to dress and act in certain ways specifically to attract men. These characteristics which include being cute, sweet, and pretty are reworded to become provocative, flirtatious, and tempting. It is worth noting that these once innocent and positive attributes are later used as damaging evidence against a woman who has been raped (Howard, 1980).

In cases where a woman is said to have "asked for it" the deter- mining factor has been her appearance and behavior. Some men in- terpret her attire and attitude as a form of speech and since "actions speak louder than words," they believe "she asked for it" and con- clude that "she deserved it." If she asked for it, then the accompany- ing beliefs are that she consented and it was not rape (Beneke, 1982). This chain reaction serves first, to condone the rape and sec- ond, to maintain the view that violence against women makes some sense in our world. If a woman chooses to go to a bar alone at night — behavior which is socially acceptable for men but not women — some men may feel that she is simply asking for trouble and ultimately will deserve whatever she gets, including rape (Beneke, 1982). This belief relieves the rapist of his crime and turns the tables around, leaving the victim to bear the responsibility of his crime against her.

Intellectually at least most people believe that sexual violence against an innocent female is inexcusable. To compensate for this inconsistency, many people have to devise some reason for its exist- ence. The just world phenomenon blames the victim for her victim- ization. Lerner (1966) suggested that many people believe that there is a positive correlation between what people do and what happens to them. By blaming the victim therefore, she gets what she deserves because we live in a just world and there needs to be a comprehensible reason for events that occur, especially those which are difficult to understand or to cope with emotionally. In this way, people can satisfy their need to maintain some faith in their own en- vironment. Lerner observed that medical students who were caring for impoverished patients expressed resentment toward these needy people. He found that the medical students held the belief that these indigent patients actually were ill because of their own carelessness and neglect and as a consequence, their poor health was actually self-inflicted. These medical students blamed innocent patients because of their own need to make sense out of a difficult situation.

Whether we are religious or not and things are not going well for us, people will ask without thinking, "why me? What have I done to deserve this?" Beneath the surface of these questions is the need to have an answer, a solution to help one live through anxious and troubling times with hope, a sense of reality and ultimately ex- planations. The powerful belief that the world is just is used to make sense out of irrational behaviors and beliefs. Jones and Aron- son (1973) conducted a study based on Lerner's theory of the just world phenomenon. A rape case was presented to college students. The only description that varied was that of the victim. In some instances she was said either to be married, a virgin or divorced. Jones and Aronson state that in our society a woman who is divorced does not receive the same respect, socially, as married women and virgins. As a consequence, they hypothesized that the subjects in their study would assign greater responsibility to rape victims who were married or virgins as opposed to divorced victims. If the world is just, then the college students would believe that married women and virgins would not be raped. However, to uphold the belief in the just world, the results indicated that when the victim was married or a virgin, the students blamed those they thought to be least at fault and the least deserving victims. By blaming the married woman and the virgin these students were able to obtain some relief from their own discomforting feelings with regard to this rape case. The reaction indicates the need to make sense out of unsettling and controversial issues.

By believing in a just world, we ease the rapist's responsibility and place a greater burden on the victim. Since sexual violence is inexcusable yet it does occur, society has had to create some reason for its existence, ergo, the just world phenomenon. What needs to be acknowledged is that rape is not only the victim's problem, but that it is equally a social problem, a problem that society as a whole must become involved with. Displaced attribution and the use of the just world phenomenon places the burden of rape on the victim alone rather than the sociopolitical arenas in our lives (Sheffield, 1984).

ATTRIBUTION OF RESPONSIBILITY

With attribution theory, people derive conclusions about their own actions and the actions of others. In this way one tries to search for reasons to understand why people act as they do. This often leads to erroneous results (Kelley, 1967). Some social psychologists (Jones, Kanouse, Kelley, Nisbett, Valins & Weiner, 1972) believe that there are three basic beliefs behind attribution theory. First and similar to the just world phenomenon is the belief that people will create causes for events which may or may not always be correct. However, by doing so they can find some personal relief. Second, people will attribute cause systematically and not randomly. And third, the results we end up with have a bearing on our emotions and actions. How one explains an event can affect their attribution of responsibility and the way they feel about the people involved. It is useful for us to study the hypotheses of Walster (1966) and Shaver (1970) with regard to the assignment of responsibility and differences in gender. Walster noted that an observer of an accident which was not severe would be likely to assign responsibility for that accident to chance or to the victim. However, in the case of a disastrous accident, Walster proposed that the assignment of responsibility would not be the same. In the case of the severe accident, one might feel great discomfort in blaming the victim or leaving the reason for the accident to chance since a similar event could occur in which the observer might be involved. Shaver hypothesized that the need to avoid negative events is connected to one's fear of being blamed for a similar event in the future of their own lives. This identity with or non-identity with the accident can have an effect on the observer's attribution of responsibility. Furthermore, Lerner's just world phenomenon restates the idea that people will get whatever they deserve because we live in a just world. Jensen and Gutek (1982) designed a study which focused on sexual harassment and assignment of responsibility. Although sexual harassment can be distinguished from rape, the results of this study can be applied to rape victims as well because the two are so closely related. They sampled 405 men and 827 women who were workers in Los Angeles County. These participants took part in the study which surveyed how men and women differed in their assignment of responsibility. Another area of their study was conducted with 135 women participants who were contacted again. All these women were victims of sexual harassment. The descriptions of their sexual harassment included:

1) While on the job, a man touched her in a sexual way.

2) The victim was expected to spend time with a man out of the workplace. It was understood that if she did not agree to go out with him, it would have a negative effect on her job, but if she did go out with him it would be in her best interest.

3) Finally, as in the latter description, the victim was expected not only to go out with a man but in some circumstances was expected to have a sexual relationship with him. Again there was the understanding that the status of her job was related to whether or not she accepted or refused him. If she was sexually involved with him, it would help her job. If she refused, her job would be negatively affected.

The study focused on the application of attribution theory in several areas in the following of which we are concerned: (a) how the assignment of responsibility for sexual harassment is affected by the difference in gender; (b) how being the victim of sexual harassment affects one's assignment of responsibility; and (c) how gender role beliefs affect the assignment of responsibility, whether the assignment of responsibility is related to one's self or to someone else. Before we continue to examine the results of the study by Jensen and Gutek, based on the theories of Walster and Shaver, Jensen and Gutek proposed that there would be different outcomes in the assignment of responsibility that men and women would make about sexual harassment. According to Shaver's theory, men would assign greater responsibility to women than would women. Based on Walster's theory, women would view women victims of sexual harassment as the responsible party. Lerner's theory invites no inequality in the attribution of responsibility. Research on rape and attribution theory (Calhoun, Selby, Cann, & Keller; 1978; Selby, Calhoun, and Brock, 1977) present Shaver's theory as an explanation for the variation in assignment of responsibility between men and women observers. Basically, men not wanting to be blamed in the future assign responsibility to women, and women too, not wanting to be blamed in the future, assign the responsibility to the men. With this in mind, let us examine the results of Jensen and Gutek study. Indeed, they found that greater responsibility was assigned to victims of sexual harassment by men. Moreover, more men than women participants supported the following statement: women usually provoke men at work and that is the reason these same men ask them to become sexually related. Generally, women will not blame women victims of sexual harassment. However, women who had not been victims themselves of sexual harassment assigned more responsibility to the women victims in this study. The results indicate that both women victims and non-victims did agree that even though there was sexual harassment on the job they could have taken some action to stop it. Women participants who had not been sexually harassed significantly endorsed this statement.

It is equally important to explore the attributions of responsibilities that victims make about themselves. Janoff-Bulman (1979) suggested that attribution theory applied to rape cases is expressed in two forms of self-blame. The first is "control related" self-blame. In this case a victim blames herself for not having taken an action that would have prevented the assault (e.g., I forgot to look behind me before I entered the lobby of my apartment house late at night to make sure I wasn't being followed). The second is "esteem related" self-blame. In this case the victim finds flaws in her own character (e.g., I am a thoughtless person) which contributed to the incident of rape. Jensen and Gutek included questions about self-blame in their study. The results indicate that the majority of victims did not evince self-blame. However, the issue of self-blame and reporting the incident of sexual harassment was also surveyed. The results demonstrated that victims of sexual harassment who also believed that they were responsible for the incident due to their own "behavioral" traits (similar to Janoff-Bulman's theory about "control-related" self-blame) were less likely to report the incident nor were they likely to talk about the incident with anyone. Those victims who internalize blame in cases of sexual assault and rape appear to be looking for the cause of the event within their own behavior. The research done in this area indicates that victims will blame themselves because they fear that others will hold them accountable for the assault and it will be used against them (Weis and Borges, 1973). Jensen and Gutek's study also revealed that those victims of sexual harassment who internalize blame for the event show a positive correlation between that self-blame and protecting the person who harassed them. Schultz (1976) reported that incidents of sexual assault are less likely to be reported if the victim and the rapist already know each other. This suggests the severity of the victim's dilemma. Hypothetically if she were a divorced woman with children, clearly the threat of losing her job could have a tremendous impact on whether or not she would report or talk with anyone at all about the incident of harassment. One might ask if the results indicated by Jensen and Gutek and Schultz indicating a positive correlation between self-blame and protecting the harasser, are not really indicative of self-blame but rather of a desperate need to keep one's job and security, thus protecting one's self due to a realistic fear. Earlier we discussed how the acceptance of rape myths in our culture served both to psychologically and socially blame the victim. Jensen and Gutek also found that there was a positive correlation between victims who believed in traditional gender roles and their assignment of responsibility. Those victims who held the belief in traditional gender roles did find women more responsible for the incident of sexual harassment. These women were likely to blame themselves and other women. On a positive note, their findings indicate that women who were victims of sexual harassment but had not adhered to gender-role stereotyped myths, were less likely to blame other women for being sexually harassed. These women indicated that they had accepted the basic beliefs of feminism and did not perpetuate the belief that sex is a man's prerogative and a woman's responsibility (Krulewitz and Nash, 1979). These results indicate that there is a salient factor which affects a victim's actions and future actions and beliefs about sexual harassment and that is, her adherence or non-adherence to gender role beliefs.

Additional support for the notion that acceptance of and the belief in traditional gender roles and how this factor affects attribution was found by Krulewitz and Payne (1977). They found that the participants who were not progressive thinkers in terms of feminism and gender roles, were less likely to call rape "rape" if there was not a significant amount of *force* used against the victim. In contrast to them were other participants whose decision about attribution of responsibility was not affected by whether or not force was used against the victim. In a similar vein, Burt and Albin (1981) conducted a study in which 598 Minnesota adults who were over the age of 18 were randomly sampled. Standard demographic questions were used to determine the participants' sex, age, education and occupation. Vignettes were used describing various rape scenes. The results of this research indicate that the incident of rape was less likely to be considered actual rape if there was a high degree of rape myth acceptance and the belief that the victim's behavior encouraged the rapist. The vignette was likely to be considered rape if it was observable that coercion was used against the victim. The latter perception showed that there was a greater chance of conviction. However, when the participants held views which were accepting of interpersonal violence, they were less likely to convict.

Thus far, we have presented research which represents victim and observer attitudes about assignment of responsibility in cases of rape and sexual harassment. These views represent victim and/or observer adherence to gender role stereotypes, acceptance of rape myths and interpersonal violence and then the conclusions that are derived at about the *victim*. In a different light, Deitz and Byrnes (1981) conducted an experiment which examined attribution of responsibility for sexual assault. The unique difference in this study is the examination of the *rapist* and his personal appearance and social status, and the impact these factors have on observer's assignment of responsibility. This study included a separate assessment of the participant's sex and his or her empathic relationship to rape victims before the trial and how this affected their attribution of responsibility. The participants included 103 women and 107 men, all college students. The experiment utilized a hypothetical rape-case and the students played the parts of "mock-jurors." The students were given two tests which were used to assess their feelings about rape and rapists. The first, the Rape Empathy Scale (RES) included twenty items each containing opposing statements which indicate total empathy toward either the rape victim or the rapist. The second test was the Rape Responsibility Questionnaire (RRS). These questions were used to obtain the participant's responses to a variety of topics some of which included: the participant's feelings about prison sentencing for the defendant, attribution of responsibility for either defendant or victim, whether or not they could identify with the victim or the rapist and their feelings about the victim and the rapist. The participants were also questioned to determine if they believed that the victim provoked the rapist, was raped due to chance, and finally, if the participants believed with assurance that the rapist was guilty. The order of the testing was as follows: 1) Rape Empathy Scale; 2) one of four vignettes describing a rape; 3) Rape Responsibility Questionnaire. The descriptions that varied in the vignettes were the defendant's occupational status and physical attractiveness. He was either an attractive or unattractive Caucasian janitor or scientist. The rape victim, a young Caucasian woman, did not vary throughout all the vignettes nor did the description of the rape incident. The results measuring the physical appearance and social status of the defendants were consistent with the hypotheses that were presented prior to this study. The results of this experiment indicate that the subjects found the *unattractive* janitor was guilty more than the *attractive* scientist. Women participants endorsed the notion that the rape victim did someting to provoke the incident and furthermore they did not identify much with the victim. The women participants assigned greater responsibility for the rape incident to the rapist and believed he was guilty. Although we are examining the rapist and his characteristics, these results appear to be consistent with the findings mentioned earlier which also indicate that male observers assign greater responsibility to the victim and women observers assign greater responsibility to the rapist. Deitz and Byrnes also found that there was a positive correlation between participants whose RES results indicate a high degree of empathy for the rape victim and extended prison terms for the defendant, concern for the victim and an identification with her. This experiment also revealed that participants with high RES scores identified more with the victim when the rapist was presented as an attractive scientist. Finally, these same high RES participants revealed that when the defendant was either attractive or unattractive they still expressed positive certainty that either was guilty more than the participants with lower RES scores. The latter were not as sure of the attractive defendant's guilt compared to the unattractive defendant's guilt. This study suggests that there is a connection between the mythology about rapists, their physical appearance and their occupational status and observer's pretrial feelings and attribution of responsibility. This highlights again, the notion that men and women do have preconceived and often erroneous beliefs about victims and rapists even before facts are presented to them. These false beliefs can affect one's attribution of responsibility and consequently the lives of both the victim and the rapist. All too often she is blamed, and he is free to roam and rape.

MASS MEDIA
AND VIOLENCE AGAINST WOMEN

It is readily apparent that we are living in a society that perpetuates and encourages rape. Sex and violence against women, gender-role stereotypes and myths are displayed in magazines, on billboards, television, film and recently T.V. videos. These commercial and everyday displays are combining sex and violence as a form of entertainment. In her new book *Science and Gender*, Ruth Bleier (1984) sums it up with a frightening account of the violences against women. These violences teach women that it is their *nature* to rely on, need and derive a sense of self-worth from men. This establishes an unequal relationship between men and women. Bleier includes violences which range from being verbally harassed, touched, physically beaten, to controlling women through the use of abortion, drugs, surgery and other unspeakable crimes. These unspeakable crimes against women are not new. The history of violence against women is nearly an endless one. However, social scientists and social psychologists have been conducting studies and research to determine what some of the factors are that contribute to the relentlessness of violence against women.

A decade ago, the Presidential Commission on Obscenity and Pornography reached the conclusion that there was not a relationship between one's exposure to erotic presentations and ensuing sexual crimes. However, currently researchers are acquiring evidence that one specific type of pornography, "aggressive-erotic" pornography, is accountable for increased men's aggression toward women. This aggression is expressed toward women in both attitudinal and behavioral changes (Trotter, 1981). Edward Donnerstein of the University of Wisconsin in Madison conducted a study to assess the effects of "aggressive-erotic" pornography and men's aggression toward women. The participants included 120 men who were college students. The students were told that this experiment was a study that had to do with the effects of stress on learning. Before viewing either a neutral, erotic or aggressive-erotic film, the participants were treated either neutrally or were made to feel anger by either a man or a woman who was an aide of the experimenter. After having viewed either one of the three films, the participants were given the chance to administer electric shocks to the fingertips of a man or a woman assistant whom they had originally encountered before viewing the film. Donnerstein debriefed the participants after the experiment and confirmed that they did indeed believe the purpose of the study was to examine the effects of stress on learning. The results of his study indicate that the students who viewed the aggressive-erotic film expressed increased aggressive behavior by giving more shocks than the participants did who viewed the erotic film. Greater aggression came from those participants who had been angered by the assistant prior to viewing the film by an aide. It is of significance to point out that the students who were originally angered by a man who was the aide and proceeded to view an aggressive erotic film did not produce more aggression than the erotic film viewers. However, the students who were originally angered by a woman aide did produce an increase in aggression only after viewing the aggressive-erotic film. In a similar vein, Neil Malamuth and James Check (1981) conducted an experiment on mass media and how they may have an effect on the acceptance of violence against women. Two hundred seventy men and women who were students served as participants to determine their reactions to the effects of exposure to films that were either violent-sexual or control films. The dependent measures were scales assessing acceptance of interpersonal violence against women, acceptance of rape myths and beliefs in adversarial sexual relations.

These participants did not view films which are considered pornographic, but rather, they viewed films which are indicative of typical movies today. The two experimental films used included *Swept
Away* and *The Getaway*. In both of these films violence against
women occurs with positive endings. The two control films used in
this study were *A Man and A Woman* and *Hooper*, neither of
which included acts of violence against women. Within a week
after viewing the movies, the students participated in a survey. The
scales were surrounded by other items on a Sexual Attitude Survey.
Participants were not aware that there was a correlation between
this survey and the films that they saw. The results indicate that the
men students were more accepting of interpersonal violence against
women and showed a trend toward rape myth acceptance. In contrast, women students exposed to the violent sexual films tended to
be less accepting of interpersonal violence and of rape myths. What
accounts for the difference between the 1970 findings by the Commission on Obscenity and Pornography and recent studies? Psychologists at the 1984 American Psychological Association Convention presented data which showed that one in eight commercial
movies released in 1983 portrayed violence against women. This is
a grave increase from 1982. The 1982 data indicated that the rate of
violence against women depicted in commercial films was one in
twenty (Goleman, 1984). It is the *content* of the pornography
which is depicting much more violence against women that is of
great concern to our well being. The images of men and women involved in sex-role, violent, stereotyped relationships, which include
the aggressive-erotic behavior acted out against women, invite the
public to accept inaccurate and dangerous displays of women and
the ways that they should be treated. Such images are not only
harmful to a woman's physical safety, but equally to her own self-
concept (Leidig, 1981). Ultimately, men and women are being exposed to radically unhealthy, abnormal models of relationships
which promote personal violence against women as acceptable and
expectable. The various sources of mass media send constant
signals throughout our culture which are reinforcing the close relationship between sex and aggression (Campbell, 1975) which further serves to encourage rape.

In a recent study at the University of New Hampshire, there has
been found a "statistically close association" between rape and pornography readership. Alaska has the highest rape rate in the United
States as well as the highest percentage of pornographic magazine

readers. Nevada, Arizona, California and Colorado ranked in the top ten for pornography readership and rape rates as well. The study was based on sales figures of eight magazines such as *Hustler* compared to the 1979 FBI crime figures (Healy, 1983).

SEX AND RAPE MYTH

Sex is the salient variable that is regularly found to be related to attitudes and beliefs about sexuality. Research demonstrates that men who were subjects will adopt rape myths and violence against women more than women (Barnett and Field, 1977; Tieger, 1981). This has led feminists to conclude that this acceptance of violence within a culture can affect whether a victim will report that she has been sexually assaulted, and how society will reach decisions of punishment for the criminal (Brownmiller, 1975; Barry, 1979; Burt, 1980; Clark, 1980). What does happen in the courtroom? As Jensen and Gutek (1982) have suggested it is most important to know which members of a jury endorse the traditional or progressive gender-role beliefs, since a jury's belief in rape myths can have a profound effect upon their decision (Borgida, 1981). The New Bedford case graphically demonstrates just how the victim of rape is put on trial. She was badgered about numerous personal issues regarding her sexual history, drinking patterns and even her relationship with her boyfriend. It was also alleged that the rape victim consented to have sex with the men and that she actually invented the incident to acquire a contract to write a book. No effort was made to ease her trauma and discomfort during the trial. She had to stand for seventeen hours and had to repeat her testimony twice. Finally, her human rights were violated again when her name appeared publicly (Beck and Zabarsky, 1984). How and why does this kind of abuse continue to exist? Whom can the rape victim turn to at a time such as this?

INCIDENCE OF RAPE

What then is rape? What might appear to be a direct question to ask and answer for some, in fact continues to generate psychological, social and political debates throughout the personal, educational and judicial aspects of our lives as individuals and as a culture. Essentially, defining rape is the crux of the problem and the critical issue in defining rape appears to be the issue of consent. At one extreme, rape is defined as all forced sex. This coercion may manifest itself psychologically, economically or physically. At the opposite end of the spectrum are those who do not acknowledge that rape exists. What falls between the two extremes is a myriad of opinions which include bits and pieces of each extreme and modifications of them. Thus far this paper has included some of the myths about rape. But what are the facts about rape? In 1983, The New York City Advisory Task Force on Rape presented some of these facts:

1) Rape is a crime of violence.

2) Women do not provoke rape nor do they want to be raped.

3) Rape does not occur for sex, but rather men rape women to dominate and humiliate them.

4) There are women who have been raped more than once; they did not provoke the rape incident on either occasion.

5) Police and government studies indicate that the way a woman is dressed or the way she behaves does not cause rape.

6) Rapists use physical violence, threats and weapons.

7) Rapists can be of all races, but non-white rapists are more likely to be prosecuted.

8) Rape is often committed by friends, relatives or acquaintances. These are people the victim already knows. This is especially true of child victims.

9) Rape is when someone does not consent.

10) Rapists violate a woman's civil rights.

11) If a woman is fortunate enough to have had some training in self-defense, she will know when it is safe to fight back.

12) All rape victims deserve support and care for surviving the incident.

The incidence of rape in the United States increases dramatically each year. Yet crimes of sexual violence are least likely to be reported. The F.B.I.'s Uniform Crime Report for 1981 shows 81,536 forcible rapes and estimates that these forcible rapes occur every six minutes. But, the National Coalition Against Sexual Assaults estimates twice as many rapes are committed each year (Rooney, 1983). There has been a 29 percent increase in forcible rapes between 1977 and 1981 (F.B.I.'s Uniform Crime Report, 1981). A study funded by the National Center for the Prevention and Control of Rape suggests that the number may be staggeringly higher, twenty-three times, or nearly two million rapes yearly (Rooney, 1983). This includes an increase in child and gang rape. It has also been estimated that nearly one-half of all rape victims are younger than twenty-five years of age and twenty-five percent of rape victims are under the age of twelve (Rush, 1980, p. 5). A United States Justice Department Study found that one-third of all rapes are committed by more than one rapist (Rooney, 1983). Other F.B.I. statistics reveal that rape is the fastest growing of the violent crimes. It is a tragedy that so often rape is not reported. Not only does the victim suffer in silence, but public, political, medical and psychological professionals are less likely to become committed to rape prevention if they are not confronted with the gravity and facts about rape. One of the problems with the enormous lack of reported rapes is that often the rape victim is overwhelmed with guilt and fear. Victims of rape fear humiliation and the horror of the consequences should they report the incident. It is estimated that between fifty-five and ninety percent of rapes are not reported (Hilberman, 1978). These statistics illustrate a problem of great magnitude, but are not surprising. Too many women, in addition to men, have accepted their place within our gender role and stereotyped culture. They harbor not only tremendous fear and guilt, but also have an added sense of responsibility for the act of rape committed against themselves. Too many rape victims remain painfully silent.

Despite the fact that rape is the fastest growing of the violent crimes, it has the lowest conviction rate of the violent crimes. Data reveal that on a national level, only one rapist out of twenty is arrested, one out of thirty is prosecuted and finally one in sixty is convicted (Geiser, 1979).

The victim who decides to report that she has been raped must be willing to undergo the additional strain of questioning and examinations that follow the actual assault. In various parts of the country, Rooney (1983) found these routine procedures take place in police stations or hospitals where the victim is confronted by cold, unsympathetic professionals. Her clothing may be taken from her and in its place she is given a hospital dressing gown. A traumatic event such as this might be ended by sending the victim home in a taxicab and later billing her for "gathering of evidence." However, if a woman decides not to report that she has been raped she might very well find herself alone, without support and care from anyone. Not only does she have to deal with feeling isolated and frightened, but she risks venereal disease and pregnancy as well as psychological manifestations of being raped. The problems include "phobic reactions, aversions to sex and depression" (Hilberman, 1978). The rape victim who has internalized gender-role myths and does believe that men are naturally dominant and aggressive responds by blaming herself rather than understanding that she has been the target and victim of some man's aggressive behavior (Herman, 1984).

AIDING THE VICTIM

Once we examine the facts about rape (without the stereotyped strings that are attached to the interpretations and consequent definitions of rape) we are most often left with a traumatized woman who has been the object of a rapist's thoroughly inhuman, illegal violation of her body. Rape appears in many forms: between married couples as well as in other relationships common today (e.g., living together, dating, friendships). This coerced sex manages to thrive because women fear violence, husbands think they have a marital right to their wives' bodies and some men still believe they are basically satisfying their "needs" (Bleier, 1984). Throughout wartime men rape women ritually and in some societies gang rape along with other forms of physical abuse including murder, has actually been approved behavior against women who did not satisfy and follow orders given to them by men. Furthermore, many young girls are never safe within their own homes since the offenders of rape and sexual abuse are often immediate family members. Moreover, because the *image* of the family needs to be upheld, many of these crimes are tucked neatly away in silence (Bleier, 1984). However, years after the actual incident many women still make connections between the assault and their daily lives, as the following quote indicates:

> "(Are you able to enjoy sex with anyone now?) It depends how I relate to the man. If I'm in a position to enjoy it — a 50-50 thing — then I'm o.k. But if I'm feeling that I'm only doing this for him and not for my own enjoyment, then I feel like the incident. . . then sex is bad." (Burgess and Holmstrom, 1981, p. 449).

Burgess and Holmstrom (1981) conducted a longitudinal study with rape victims which focused on sexual disruption and recovery. Some of the results indicated that the majority of victims decreased their sexual activity, some actually abstaining for at least six months from having sexual relations, or longer. Many victims experience flashbacks to the actual incident as well as pain and discomfort during sexual intercourse. Other results indicated that rape victims were worried about their partners' feelings. What about her feelings? Rape leaves a woman with feelings of guilt, anger, helplessness, worthlessness, uncleanliness, mistrust, depression, a loss of sexual interest, isolation, moodiness, and fears of the night, crowds and men. Victims experience numerous painful (and unimaginable for most of us) post-rape psychological, physical, and social problems. Often women who have been raped experience changes in all aspects of their lives ranging from their eating and sleeping habits, increased nightmares and fears of being home alone, to worsened heterosexual relationships and low self-esteem with regard to their sexual attractiveness (McCahill, Meyer and Fischman, 1979).

There are several factors which contribute to a rape victim's post-rape adjustment including her age, whether or not she is single, married, divorced, widowed or what her employment status is. Those victims living with family members are more likely to receive emotional support. However, married women are often blamed for the rape. This would be consistent with the mythology that she must have provoked the rapist or else she would have been able to fight him off. Recovery for the rape victim can also depend on the details of the rape. One of the most devastating realities of brutal rape for the rape victim is that she is confronted with the possibility of her own death (e.g., being choked, threatened by rapist with a weapon). These experiences are bound to cause major adjustment problems which can vary with each individual woman and her experience. Other problems arise for the rape victim whose route to and from work is the same as or similar to the environment in which she was raped. In this situation rape victims are likely to experience tremendous anxiety. Furthermore, adjustment problems arise for women who prior to being raped had low self-esteem. These victims are likely to blame themselves for the incident (McCahill, Meyer and Fischman, 1979).

Unfortunately rape not only affects the rape victim but many of the people close to and around her. If the victim is indeed a victim of her own sex-role stereotyped beliefs, what can be done to enlighten her and ease her fears, guilt and lack of knowledge about rape? Women need to be informed about rape prevention and provided with information and skills for self-protection. Women of all ages need to know that they are entitled to feel an endless range of emotions ranging from rage to depression. However, in treating the victim of rape, clinicians need to remember that an incident of rape is a personal and traumatizing experience for each and every woman in her own way. All kinds of rape, brutal rape, rapes with weapons, rapes committed by strangers, rapes between acquaintances (McCahill, Meyer and Fischman, 1979) need to be examined in and of themselves since all rapes can manifest adjustment problems of unique proportions for each rape victim.

Rape victims are helped to regain their sense of worth and locus of control by talking, if they choose to, about their experience in a non-judgmental atmosphere. Services are offered to rape victims in a variety of ways some of which include rape hot-line counseling, support groups and in-person counseling and psychotherapy. Certain considerations are useful to make in counseling rape victims. Initially it is helpful to determine whom she trusts, would feel comforted and supported by, and to try to involve these people in caring for her. In this way she is guaranteed safety and a sense of security. If the rape victim is especially traumatized the counselor may need to be available for her at almost any time. On the other hand, some victims may need extra encouragement to express their feelings. Due to the complexity of the roles some women are fulfilling today, rape victims may need help coping with their full lifestyles. Young women still living at home may have to confront their parents, married women have to confront not only their spouses but also their children, older women may have a greater amount of difficulty openly communicating their feelings with a therapist and finally, all women will have to deal with their feelings about themselves.

In just a few short lines of poetry, a young woman in her twenties sheds some light on her own struggle to mature and survive the incident of rape that she experienced:

> "Again, a philosophy I have temporarily
> finalized. Very much alive in today, I
> write this of yesterday so I may live
> tomorrow:
> *EMOTIONAL DEATH*
> I get hurt and I get crushed
> Then I vow to never again
> And keeping my inner feelings hushed
> I smile with myself in pain."
> Anonymous, 1975

It is essential for us to continue to do research in order to discover positive, healthy ways to give the rape victim the support and care she needs to regain self-esteem and a sense of control over her life. This research must include methods by which we can reach the minds of so many people who exist in a world filled with erroneous beliefs about behavior in both men and women. Timothy Beneke is quite right when he says that "if violence is to end, we need nothing less than a revolution in the consciousness among men" (1982, p. 33).

CONCLUSION

Despite the fact that rape is gravely prevalent within our culture, it does not have to occur. In a cross-cultural survey Peggy Sanday (1981) found that cultures with a high incidence of rape accepted interpersonal violence and men's domination of women and encouraged the separation of men and women. Conversely, Sanday found that societies which had a low incidence of rape were characterized by sexual equality. Although these societies are small in number they did not have gender-role stereotyped behavior, interpersonal violence between the sexes nor a high incidence of rape, suggesting that rape-free societies can exist.

Most men and women can understand that women fear rape at various moments in assorted places throughout their lives. At an early age the fear of rape is instilled in young girls in their own best interest. Yet, while women are taught to be fearful and concerned about rape, why has the issue of rape mainly been a woman's problem (Bleier, 1984)? The commonness and availability of aggressive pornography is rampant. Even men who genuinely possess caring, feminist thinking and behavior have just as great a struggle to create a climate of concern for the rape victim. They have to contend with the rest of the male culture that survives on the domination of women.

We have an overwhelming need for education which teaches us all the truths about rape. We need to explore healthy, honest ways of communicating the realities about rape, especially to our children before they too become the expressors of "falsehoods" about rape and sex-role behaviors and attitudes. We need to implement textbooks, storybooks, movies, advertising and other forms of mass media which provide us with examples of women and men who are both free to achieve equal status (physically, economically and emotionally) and respect. With this education we can hope to create space for healthy human relationships. To achieve this kind of harmony, we need to envision, grasp, and hold on to the belief that true equality between the sexes can rid us of the fears, incidence and ultimately existence of rape.

REFERENCES

Anonymous. (1975).

Barnett, N.J., & Field, H. (1977). Sex differences in university students' attitudes toward rape. *Journal of College Student Personnel, 2,* 93–96.

Barry, K. (1979). *Female sexual slavery.* Englewood Cliffs, New Jersey: Prentice Hall.

Beck, M., & Zabarsky, M. (1984, April 2). Rape trial: 'Justice crucified'? *Newsweek,* p. 39.

Beneke, T. (1982). *Men on rape.* New York: St. Martin's Press.

Bleier, R. (1984). *Science and gender.* New York: Pergamon Press.

Borgida, E. (1981). Legal reform of rape laws. In L. Bickman (Ed.), *Applied social psychology annual* (Vol. 2, pp. 211–242). Beverly Hills, Ca: Sage.

Brownmiller, S. (1975). *Against our will: Men, women and rape.* New York: Simon & Schuster.

Burgess, A.W., & Holmstrom, L.L. (1981). Rape: Sexual disruption and recovery. In E. Howell & M. Bayes (Eds.), *Women and mental health* (pp. 449–461). New York: Basic Books, Inc.

Burt, M.R. (1980). Cultural myths and supports for rape. *Journal of Personality and Social Psychology, 38,* 217–230.

Burt, M.R., & Albin, R.S. (1981, May–June). Rape myths, rape definitions and probability of conviction. *Journal of Applied Social Psychology, 11,* 212–230.

Calhoun, L.G., Selby, J.W., Cann, A., & Keller, G.T. (1978). The effects of victim physical attractiveness and sex of respondents on social reactions to victims of rape. *The British Journal of Social and Clinical Psychology, 17,* 191–192.

Campbell, P.B. (1975). Are we encouraging rape? *Crisis Intervention, 6*(4), 20–27.

Clark, L. (1980). Pornography's challenge to liberal ideology. *Canadian Forum, 3,* 9–12.

Clark, L. & Lewis, D. (1977). *Rape: The price of coercive sexuality,* Canada: The Women's Press.

Deitz, S.R., & Byrnes, L.E. (1981, May). Attribution of responsibility for sexual assault: The influence of observer empathy and defendant occupation and attractiveness. *Journal of Psychology, 108* (1), 17–29. ,

Dullea, G. (1979, September 4). Child prostitution: Causes are sought (p. C11). *The New York Times.*

Geiser, R.L. (1979). *Hidden victims: The sexual abuse of children.* Boston: Beacon Press.

Goleman, D. (1984, August). Violence against women in films. *The New York Times,* pp. C1, C5.

Healy, Michelle. (1983, December). Pornography readership linked to rape rates. *USA Today,* p. 30.

Herman, D. (1984). The rape culture. In J. Freeman (Ed), *Women: A feminist perspective* (pp. 20–38). Palo Alto, CA: Mayfield Publishing Co.

Hilberman, E. (1978). The impact of rape. In M.T. Notman & C.C. Nadelson (Eds.), *The women patient: Medical & psychological interfaces* (pp. 303–323). New York: Plenum.

Howard, J. (1980). Battered and raped — the physical/sexual abuse of women. In F. Delacoste & F. Newman (Eds.) *Fight back! Feminist resistance to male violence.* (pp. 71–84). Minnesota: Cleis Press.

Janoff-Bulman, R. (1979). Characterological versus behavioral self-blame: Inquiries into depression and rape. *Journal of Personality & Social Psychology, 37,* 1798–1809.

Jensen, I.W., & Gutek, B.A. (1982). Attributions & assignments of responsibility in sexual harassment. *Journal of Social Issues, 38* (4).

Jones, C., & Aronson, E. (1973). Attribution of fault to a rape victim as a function of respectability of the victim. *Journal of Personality and Social Psychology, 23,* 415–419.

Jones, E.E., Kanouse, D.E., Kelley, H.H., Nisbett, R.E., Valins, S., & Weiner, B. (1972). *Attribution: Perceiving the causes of behavior.* Morristown, New Jersey: General Learning Press.

Kanekar, S., & Kolsawalla, M.B. (1977). Responsibility in relation to respectability. *Journal of Social Psychology, 102,* 183–188.

Kanekar, S., & Kolsawalla, M.B. (1980). Responsibility of rape victim in relation to her respectability. *Journal of Social Psychology, 112,* 153–154.

Kelley, H.H. (1967). Attribution theory in social psychology. In D. Levine (Ed.), *Nebraska Symposium on Motivation,* (Vol. 15, pp. 192–238). Lincoln: University of Nebraska Press.

Krulewitz, J.E. & Nash, J.E. (1979). Effects of rape victim resistance, assault outcome, and sex of observer on attributions about rape. *Journal of Personality, 47,* (4), 557–574.

Krulewitz, J.E., & Payne, E.J. (1977). Sex differences in attribution about rape, rapists and rape victims. Paper presented at the meeting of the American Psychological Association, San Francisco.

Leidig, M.W. (1981). Violence against women: A feminist-psychological analysis. In S. Cox (Ed.), *Psychology of the emerging self* (pp. 190–205). New York: St. Martin's Press.

Lerner, M.J. (1966, September). The unjust consequences of the need to believe in a just world. Paper presented at the meeting of the American Psychological Association, New York.

Malamuth, N.M., Haber, S. & Feshbach, S. (1980). Testing hypothesis regarding rape: Exposure to sexual violence, sex differences, and the "normality" of rapists. *Journal of Research in Personality, 14,* 121–137.

Malamuth, N.M. & Check, J.V. (1981, December). The effects of mass media exposure on acceptance of violence against women: A field experiment. *Journal of Research in Personality, 15* (4), 436–446.

McCahill, T.W., Meyer, L.C., & Fischman, A.M. (1979). *The aftermath of rape.* Toronto: Lexington Books.

McCaldon, R.J. (1967). Rape. *Canadian Journal of Corrections, 9,* 37–59.

Medea, A. & Thompson, K. (1974). *Against rape.* New York: Farrar, Straus & Giroux.

Palm, R. & Abrahamsen, D. (1954). A Rorschach study of the wives of sex offenders. *Journal of Nervous and Mental Diseases, 119,* 167–172.

Rooney, R. (1983, September). Rape the battle of the sexes turns violent. *The Ladies Home Journal,* pp. 87–89 & 140–145.

Rush, F. (1980). *The best kept secret.* Englewood Cliffs, New Jersey: Prentice Hall.

Sanday, P.R. (1981). The social-cultural context of rape: A cross-cultural study. *Journal of Social Issues, 37* (4), 5–27.

Schultz, L. (1976). *Rape victimology.* Springfield, Ill: Charles C. Thomas.

Selby, J.W., Calhoun, L.G., & Brock, T. (1977). Sex differences in the social perception of rape victims. *Personality and Social Psychology Bulletin, 3,* 412–415.

Shaver, K.G. (1970). Defensive attribution: Effects of severity and relevance on the responsibility assigned to accidents. *Journal of Personality and Social Psychology, 14,* 101–113.

Sheffield, C.J. (1984). Sexual terrorism. In J. Freeman (Ed.), *Women: A feminist perspective* (pp. 3–19). Palo Alto, CA: Sage.

Tieger, T. (1981). Self-rated likelihood of raping and the social perception of rape. *Journal of Research in Personality, 15,* 147–154.

Trotter, R. (1980, September 13). Sex and violence: Pornography hurts. *Science News,* pp. 166, 172.

United States Department of Justice, Federal Bureau of Investigation (1981). *Crime in the United States Uniform Crime Report.* Washington, D.C.: Government Printing Office.

Walster, E. (1966). Assignment of responsibility for an accident. *Journal of Personality and Social Psychology, 3,* 73–79.

Watson, D.L., deBortali-Tregerthan, D., & Frank, J. (1984). *Social psychology: Science and application.* Glenview, Ill: Scott, Foresman & Co.

Weis, K., & Borges, S. (1973). Victimology and rape: The case of the legitimate victim. *Issues in Criminology, 8,*(20), 71–114.

HOMO ECONOMICUS AS THE RAPIST IN SOCIOBIOLOGY

Julia Siegel Schwendinger
AND
Herman Schwendinger

INTRODUCTION

Although no biological theory of crime has received systematic support from empirical research, the belief in evolutionary biological theories persists and, in recent years, an apparently new perspective, "sociobiology," has emerged. This perspective has been stimulated by reports of striking behavioral similarities between humans, primates and other sentient beings, even though these beings are otherwise entirely different. Following up on these analogous relationships, sociobiologists insist that primates and human beings are motivated by the same instincts. Among primates, these instinctual imperatives create a never-ending struggle for dominance among individuals, male domination of females, and violence against outsiders. For humans, these same aggressive, dominant-submissive, and territorial imperatives encourage such things as social classes, gender inequality and war.

One might reasonably object that sociobiological analogies ignore the extraordinary complexities of human society such as the economic, political and symbolic relationships that differentiate humans from other living things. In light of these complexities, analogous connections between two enraged gorillas and a modern World War seem quite superficial. But sociobiologists regard such complexities as theoretically unimportant. It is the analogy that counts even for the study of criminal behavior.

In the last few years, the search for analogies has reached unprecedented proportions especially among sociobiological theorists of *rape*. These theorists make the surprising claim that sexually assaultive behavior is by no means confined to humans and primates. According to these theorists, studies now show that those beautiful mallard ducks rape. Rapists can also be found among bullfrogs, spawning longear sunfish, pied flycatchers, south American leaf fish, bank swallows, and acanthocephalan worms. Alas, even the lovely bluebirds rape. (See Harding's chapter in this monograph). Consequently, sociobiologists claim there are genetic relationships which force members of one species after another to sexually assault their fellow creatures. It is further reasoned that rape has been encouraged by evolutionary biological processes. It is produced by natural selection because it is adaptive behavior that results in greater reproductive success. Rape occurs because it enables a male entity to reproduce himself by passing on his genes.

Although there is some mention of proximate causes such as life experience and social milieu, the evolutionary factors are emphasized as being the *ultimate* causes. Rape, therefore, is fundamentally a product of natural and not psychological, social, economic and political relationships.

SOCIAL DARWINIAN
PRECURSORS OF SOCIOBIOLOGY

Such a perspective toward criminal behavior is not without historical antecedents. It by no means represents the first attempt to explain crime on the basis of biological evolution, population growth, heredity, or natural selection. Social Darwinists in the nineteenth century had already made these analytic categories into plausible candidates for explaining crime as well as other harmful human relationships. To show their contribution in this context, we will briefly review writings by Malthus and Spencer and then examine modern theories of rape in greater detail.

Discussions of social Darwinian theories begin with Malthus (1914). He asserts that all "plants and irrational animals . . . are impelled by a powerful instinct to the increase of their species." The human species also possesses the instinct to propagate, but unlike all other forms of life, Malthus notes that the human species is capable of doubling its population every twenty-five years. Since the increase is not kept in check among humans by limitations in available land and food, the population will rapidly outstrip the available food supply. Therefore, Malthus says that unless the population is held in check by certain "natural forces," millions of people throughout the world will be "totally unprovided for." The natural forces inexorably limiting population growth, according to Malthus, include crime as well as "all unwholesome occupations, severe labor and exposure to the seasons, extreme poverty, bad nursing of children . . . the whole train of common diseases and epidemics, wars, plague and famine." (p. 13–14). These forces especially eliminate people from the lower classes.

Surprisingly, even though most of these forces appear to be commanded by human beings and even though they seem to be produced by human institutions, they are nevertheless considered to be forces of nature fundamentally independent of human will.

Herbert Spencer, not Charles Darwin, is the central figure in the development of social Darwinism but his natural selection theory is influenced by Malthusian ideas. In "A Theory of Population, Deduced from the General Law of Animal Fertility," Spencer (1852) paradoxically asserts that the same imbalance in population and food that creates war, crime, famine, and epidemics also has positive effects: it brings about moral improvements in people, increases human intelligence, and decreases the rate of population growth. This all comes about through evolutionary processes. Spencer proposes that the forward march of civilization is due to population pressures that force people to abandon individualistic predatory habits and take up agriculture and industry. By making more complex social organization inevitable, these pressures favor the development of *biological adaptations* with greater intelligence and social sentiments. Concurrently, the destructive natural checks on the population continue to eliminate less intelligent and sexually irresponsible members of the race because they are less *adaptive* than others. According to Spencer, these two trends are increasing the average intelligence and moral qualities of the species as a whole.

Spencer's theory is critically dependent upon a biological mechanism effected by *natural selection*. (This mechanism is especially important because we will compare it with sociobiological mechanisms). Equating an increase in intelligence with greater growth of the brain and other parts of the nervous system, and an increase in fertility with greater growth of the reproductive system, Spencer (1852) proposes that the nervous and reproductive systems of individuals compete for the same fund of "phosphorous," "neurine" (p. 492), and other nutrient elements. Because of this competition, an increase in the intellectual status of the species can only take place at the expense of its ability to propagate at previous rates. Therefore, although it was originally responsible for stimulating social organization and human intelligence, population pressure would eventually disappear with this very development. "The pressure of population, as it gradually finishes its work," Spencer concludes, "must gradually bring itself to an end" (p. 501). And happily, the miseries (such as crime and war) accompanying population pressure will also disappear.

Around the turn of the 20th century, criminology was strongly influenced by Spencer. Cesare Lombroso, for instance, adopted Spencer's notion that social sentiments improved as humanity evolved biologically. He theorized that some people were "born criminals" because they were "atavistic throwbacks" whose biological traits were similar to the traits of predatory "savage races" at lower stages of biological evolution. Epilepsy also made people criminal, Lombroso said. It caused the degeneration of the nervous system and hence the development of atavistic characteristics. Atavistic criminals were identifiable because they were more likely to be mentally retarded, sexually improvident, unable to empathize with others or subscribe to higher moral values. Atavism was also suggested by a small cranial capacity, dark skin pigmentation, broad noses, and tufted or crispy hair, and so forth.

Lombrosian theory went into sharp decline when it was falsified by empirical research. However, the social impact of social Darwinism, as a general perspective, did not depend on the scientifically verifiable status of any particular application. Despite its fallacious status, social Darwinism had an extraordinary effect on social thinking (Hofstadter, 1959). This effect, as we shall note later, was partly due to its conservative ideology and political perspective.

Throughout the United States, social Darwinism supported academic schools of thought that attributed one social problem after another to biological evolution, the nature of humans, processes of natural selection, and the pressures of population. In addition, in the later 20th century, the great strides made by genetic theorists in biology also began to influence social Darwinian theories. We shall soon see, however, that the geneticists' influence is most evident in the biological *images* and *metaphors* rather than the biological mechanisms employed by sociobiologists. Furthermore, once the facade of biological metaphors and images is penetrated, we discover the mechanisms that really drive sociobiological theories. *These mechanisms are not shaped by biological propositions.* They are composed entirely of psychological and economic ideas which are derived from simple utilitarian propositions and classical economic theory. Let us describe two sociobiological theories of rape to make these points.

WHO COMMITS THE CRIME?
MR. GENES, THE BUTLER, OR
HOMO ECONOMICUS, THE MERCHANT?

In one of these theories, Shields and Shields (1983) state that the biological impulse to rape is produced by millions of years of genetic programming favored by natural selection. These scholars add, "We suspect that during human evolutionary history, males that possessed a mating strategy that included rape as a facultative response were favored by natural selection over those that did not" (p. 123). Biological evolution through natural selection has established rape as a reproductive strategy for men.

However, since rape victims rarely report hearing reproductive desires expressed by rapists, this function appears to be unconscious. Rapists often make their wishes and attitudes known: "I want to screw you!" "Eat me!" "You're a slut!" — but they are rarely known to say, "I want you to get pregnant." In fact, the Shields suggest that the reproductive function of rape operates at an unconscious level. Regarding goals and decision-making connected with rape, they point out that this "is not meant to imply conscious decision-making in any animal, including humans. Rather such decisions are expected to be *programmed* (our emphasis) by natural selection . . ." (p. 117).

Rape as a reproductive strategy in sociobiological theory is not the sole approach taken by males. There are at least two alternative strategies: honest courtship — the primary strategy — and deceitful or manipulative courtship where the male does not intend to provide the necessary paternal investment. Rape does occur however where the *benefits* are potentially high and the costs are low. According to Shields and Shields, "Rape is expected to occur only when its potential benefit (production of an extra offspring) exceeds its potential cost (energy expended and risk taken owing to some probability of resistance or retribution that would reduce a rapist's success)" (p. 115).

Besides costs and benefits, a further limitation on the prevalence of rape is the type of male involved. A second theory (Thornhill and Thornhill, 1983) proposes that "human rape is an evolved facultative alternative that is primarily employed when *men are unable to compete* (our emphasis) for resources and status necessary to attract and reproduce with desirable mates" (p. 137). It is necessary for men to compete because polygyny is part of human evolutionary history. The resulting shortage of desirable women — the best are monopolized by high status men — is a condition requiring rape as a strategy.

Now scholars have undoubtedly been struck by the novelty of theories purporting to show that men, bullfrogs, bluebirds and worms share biological traits that make them violate the most elementary rules of conduct. Given such similarities, moreover, one should reasonably expect these theories to reveal some grand biological mechanism previously unknown to science in this context. Spencer's theory certainly provides such a mechanism. As indicated, in his theory, fertility rates are determined by the relative sizes of two types of cells which compete for the same limited fund of nutrients. An increase in intellectual cells lowers the propagation rates and the growth of the other cells increases propagation rates. As biological evolution produces a greater number of people with higher intelligence, the population pressure and its harmful consequences are lowered. This mechanism clearly grounds Spencer's theory in biological processes — even though it is pure fiction. The causal propositions in sociobiological theories refer to different levels of reality, the biological level and the social. What kinds of propositions illuminate their biological relationships?

Unfortunately, when the biological propositions are scrutinized, an enormous explanatory gap appears. After the analogies with other species are drawn and once rape is vaguely attributed to biological evolution, natural selection and genetic programming, the strictly biological propositions about human beings suddenly cease. The genetic process underlying rape seems to be taken for granted, and the genetic components of this process are not actually described. The same vanishing act applies to statements about the higher nervous system. Thornhill and Thornhill (1983) state, for in-

stance, that "[A male's] decisions regarding adoption of alternatives are based ultimately upon their value to his reproduction. . . .
In an ultimate sense his evaluation stems from mechanisms of perception and decision-making in his nervous system that were
favored by natural selection in human evolutionary history" (p.
164). But the authors provide no description of the *concrete* nature
of these "mechanisms of perception and decision-making" in a
man's nervous system.

Thus, sociobiological theories are considered an alternative to
social science theories because they claim that rape is caused by
evolutionary biological processes. But the propositions that play
the most critical role in differentiating sociobiological theories con-
sist largely of biological metaphors and vague references to biological processes. While rape may be considered a "reproductive strategy" favored by "genetic programming" and "natural selection," the
sociobiologists do not actually provide the biological mechanisms
revealing the nature of this programming. Neither do they provide
a convincing biological explanation for the adaptability of strategies based on "honest courtship and marriage" or seduction. Human
propagation has occurred in a variety of social contexts (e.g., band
society, nuclear family, slave brothels, joint family groups) and the
differences between these contexts often seem unrelated to their
adaptability for genetic survival. What is the nature of the *human
biological programming* that produces courtship, seduction and
rape as reproductive strategies? The sociobiologists do not answer
this question. Until a verifiable answer is provided, their biological
propositions are purely speculative.

On the other hand, whereas sociobiologists have little to say
about biological processes, they provide detailed explanations of
choice-making behavior resulting in rape. These explanations are
drawn from simple utilitarianism and classical economic theory —
not biology. The utilitarian (pleasure-pain) premises underlying
their "cost-benefit" analysis are quite familiar and do not have to be
described. Our reference to classical economic theory, on the other
hand, may not be as familiar. In addition to utilitarian propositions, classical economic theory is associated with "the scarcity postulate," a formal description of how people make rational choices
when their means are limited. Choice-making behavior in this context requires comparisons that identify the means with "a maximum
use value." Thus, an investor with a limited amount of money com-
pares the return, the interest or profit, produced by alternative in-

vestments to find an investment with the greatest return. In economic theory, this choice-making behavior is called "economizing behavior."

Utilitarian and economistic ideas obviously underlie sociobiological theories of rape. To maximize return, i.e., the number of offspring, males with limited opportunities (means) make alternative choices. Thornhill and Thornhill (1983) assert, for example, that "on reaching adulthood, [a male] is expected to shift from alternatives of lower reproductive return to alternatives of higher reproductive return depending on available opportunities [resources]" (p. 164). In Thornhill and Thornhill's theory, some men engage in rape because they have too few resources to propagate honestly. These men switch to "a big winner alternative . . . that will be more reproductively profitable than other alternatives" (p. 139). Given their limitations, rape, as a reproductive strategy, has maximum use value. It is most profitable.

Without authentic biological mechanisms, the plausibility of sociobiological theories is therefore largely dependent on the intellectual climate established by modern social Darwinians (Ardrey, 1966; Lorenz, 1966) and the popularity of utilitarian and classical economic ideas. In Shields' and Thornhills' theories, the biological metaphors veil commonly used economic models. Classical economic ideas, however, can and do play an independent role in rape theories. This independent role is illustrated by another theory of rape developed by Clark and Lewis (1977). Their theory employs similar utilitarian and economic notions for explaining rape, yet it is not a sociobiological theory.

Clark and Lewis propose that men employ the same strategies for gaining sexual matings as the sociobiologists. However, Clark and Lewis' theory only utilizes economic causal propositions. These authors propose that men regard women as owners of salable sexual properties: "From the male point of view female sexuality is a commodity in the possession of women, even if it is something men will come to own and control under the appropriate circumstances" (p. 128-129). Thus, female sexuality is bought and sold in an open market where men are buyers and women are sellers. However, the market is dominated by masculine conceptions of property and therefore the best bargain a woman can achieve is still limited. Furthermore, when bargaining for sex, men may either select the option of paying the cost of marriage, if their offer is accepted, or they may use various forms of coercion. They may make promises they cannot or will not really fulfill. They may harass women or threaten them with physical harm or rape them.

The independence of the economistic propositions about choice-making behavior is further illustrated by Clark and Lewis' theory. Also notice the similarity between their market model theory and the sociobiological one. After describing their market model, they state, "The tactic of coercion which a man uses will depend on the personal assets which he has on hand." Men who have money and other resources can drive a bargain in their own interests easily. Other men — who are ugly, perhaps, but certainly if they are poor — will take sex from women by force, because they have no other means of driving a bargain. These men "lack the necessary social and economic means of acquiring it legitimately" (p. 129-130). Obviously, the economistic propositions underlying the Thornhills' theory are virtually identical with the Clark and Lewis' propositions.

As indicated, once sociobiological propositions are examined carefully, the references to choice-making behavior which make them credible are composed of shopworn, commonsensical, utilitarian and economistic ideas which have been applied to an extraordinary variety of criminal acts for almost two hundred years. The ideas oversimplify psychological processes underlying criminal behavior and they have been least successful in explanations of violent behavior.

FEMINISM AND NEW THEORIES OF RAPE

Some of the major alternatives to sociobiology today have been influenced by feminists. In the early 1970s when the social and political impact of feminist movements exploded on the American scene, the crime of rape became a master symbol of women's oppression. At first, most feminists agreed with traditional schools of thought which assumed that women were oppressed because of the inherent nature of men. Gradually, however, some feminists, in broadening their focus, questioned the universality of rape. They tied rape into psychological, sociological and anthropological relationships that occur in some societies and not others. They argued that violence against women was related to *sexual inequality* and that both of these relationships had nothing to do with the *instincts* for power and aggression inherent in men.

For instance, social scientists are now contesting the notion that women everywhere and at all times have been placed in an inferior position to men. This is important to our argument because inferior status correlates with rape. Although conventional anthropologists have largely ignored women's independence in societies existing in the recent past, a feminist trend is now calling for the reexamination of ethnographic data about women's status. Mina Caulfield (1977), Ruby Rohrlich-Leavitt, Barbara Sykes, and Elizabeth Weatherford (1975), Eleanor Leacock (1981) and Peggy Sanday (1981) and others suggest that women in some societies should now be considered far more independent than they have been made out to be. They insist that traditional studies of these women are based on culturally biased observations made especially but not exclusively by anthropologists who were men. The studies have projected androcentric biases onto observations of tribal relations and, as a result, they discount and distort the role of women. Women's dignity, independent thinking, rituals, and associations are ignored. In these traditional studies, evidence of egalitarian relations is minimized while the spheres of masculine domination are exaggerated.

Efforts by less conventional anthropologists to discover existent egalitarian societies have begun to pay off. A study in 1978 of the Agta, a Negrito people of the Philippines, by Agnes Estioko-Griffin and P. Bion Griffin (1981), discovered continuing egalitarian relations. After a well-specified definition of equality, the authors concluded: "The case must be rested that Agta women are equal to men. They do have authority, and they do regularly contribute a significant portion of the subsistence resources. Their freedom of choice in sex and marriage seems to support the hypothesis of an egalitarian society" (p. 140).

Colin Turnbull (1981) presents another exception to androcentric anthropology, finding, among the Mbuti, no sense of "superordination or subordination" (p. 219) between the genders but rather an emphasis on interdependence. He says: "Plainly then, 'Womanhood,' for the Mbuti, is associated with motherhood, and indeed both men and women see themselves as equal in all respects except the supremely vital one that, whereas the woman can (and on occasion does) do everything the male does, she can do one thing no male can do: give birth to life" (p. 206).

The recently discovered Tasaday, a Stone Age people living in a Philippine rain forest, provide still another example of egalitarian and non-violent relationships. John Nance (1975) writes about the Tasaday's social relations: "Younger children were constantly carried, held, nuzzled, caressed; older Tasaday spoke together warmly, touched gently, shared food and shelter with no trace of friction" (p. 25). The Tasaday demonstrated "no greed, no selfishness . . . They share everything" (p. 75). They also had little hierarchical structure; decision making was "based on discussions in which men and women expressed views equally, with age and experience determining degrees of influence" (p. 24). All their interactions seem rooted in love.

Gender equality and lack of violence are considered causally important by Peggy Sanday who conducted one of the most important studies of rape in recent years. Sanday (1981) examined anthropological observations of 95 societies, in the Human Relations Area Files, because they contained information about rape. The societies which were selected from a larger sample, were divided into relatively "rape-free" and "rape-prone" societies. Almost half of the reports (47 percent) were represented by rape-free societies where rape was absent or rare. Less than a quarter (17 percent) proved to be unambiguously rape-prone because the members of these societies either displayed the social use of rape to threaten or punish women or had a high incidence of rape of their own or other women. Reports of rape existed for the remaining 36 percent but the incidence is not known. Comparing the rape-prone societies with the rape-free societies, Sanday emphasized that the rape-prone societies were characterized by a marked degree of gender inequality. Other shared characteristics were a greater toleration of violence, glorification of aggression by men, and competitiveness. Women in the rape-free societies were respected influential members of their communities. Their societies were less violent and men were gentle and cooperative. Sanday concluded that rape is bred in an atmosphere of violence and it is not determined by the inherent nature of human beings. Rape, other forms of violence, and gender inequality are expressions of cultural relationships that develop under certain social conditions.

Since gender inequality is a causal factor in rape, let us examine it more closely. The search for social conditions that breed such inequality has been conducted for a century and a half by evolutionary *social* theorists. Today, these theorists point out that gender inequality is not a monolithic phenomenon. Societies are characterized by degrees of gender equality or inequality. Moreover, even within very inegalitarian societies women's status may vary from one social sphere to another. Keeping this in mind, Karen Sacks (1975) analyzed gender inequality and socioeconomic relationships in four societies, the Mbuti, Lovedu, Mpondo and Ghanda. The Mbuti and Ghanda respectively represented the most gender egalitarian and the most gender inegalitarian societies. The Lovedu were generally egalitarian whereas the Mpondo were inegalitarian but, within each of these societies, women's status depended on the social context. This status varied somewhat depending on whether it was expressed in regard to the immediate household, property relationships, political life and so forth.

Studies by Sacks and others indicate that societies with higher degrees of gender equality are also characterized by particular kinds of *socioeconomic* relations. Relatively egalitarian societies frequently have economies based on hunting and gathering food or on horticulture, which are pursued chiefly for collective use and not for commercial exchange. The Tasaday, for instance, survive on hunting and gathering food. Their economy is based on the communal production of use values, and their only exchange is informal gift trading with the single native outsider who visits them occasionally. The Arapesh economy, on the other hand, depends on agricultural pursuits such as gathering breadfruit, growing taro, banana, and tobacco plants, raising pigs as well as hunting game. Nevertheless, the gardening, hunting, house building, and other activities are chiefly communal enterprises, and Arapesh trade is a form of informal gift exchange. Cooperation and sharing are strongly emphasized in work and ideology. Such societies tend to be characterized by little or no sexual violence because, under these socioeconomic conditions, relations between women and men are cooperative and compassionate (Mead, 1963).

According to Eleanor Leacock (1975), there have been numerous other agricultural or nomadic people whose households were communal. Here gender equality predominated and the division of labor between the sexes was reciprocal. Among such tribes, women restricted their own activities if their mobility was limited by pregnancy, infirmity, or the nursing of infants. Understandably, others who were handicapped, physically or by age, women or men had similar restrictions. Otherwise, although there was a gender division of labor, large collective hunts including men and women were quite common. Also, women took small game alone and men likewise did some food gathering. In addition, it is believed that women's autonomy and their close supportive relations with men were cardinal features of prehistoric societies.

Speaking about economic relations in these societies, Leacock (1975) emphasizes the independence and mobility of wives: "[Their] economy did not involve the dependence of the wife and children on the husband." She adds, "Women did not have to put up with personal injuries from men in outbursts of violent anger for fear of economic privation for themselves or their children" (p. 33). Unlike women today, some of whom are bound (without protection from relatives and friends) to brutal husbands, a woman in these societies at the very least could call on her relatives for redress. If amends were not made, she could leave freely and return to her own family.

Descriptions of life in these societies are conspicuously devoid of the repeated violence against women expressed in the United States. The indifference to violence involving persons other than oneself is also conspicuously absent. In fact, in these societies a rapist's own family might move against him to rectify his wrong. Stanley Diamond (1971), an authority on custom and law, examined punishments for rape in Dahomey. He notes that "if rape had, in fact, occurred in the joint-family villages — and such an occurrence *would have been rare* [our emphasis] . . . the wrong could have been dealt with by composition (the ritualized giving of goods to the injured party), ritual purification, ridicule, and perhaps, for repeated transgression, banishment; the customary machinery would have gone into effect automatically, probably on the initiative of the family of the aggressor" (p. 41).

Gender inequality and rape also seem to be correlated with other forms of violence against women. However, the connections between (1) rape and other forms of violence against women and (2) theories of gender inequality are complex because the development of this inequality itself changes from one society to another depending on historical circumstances. There are at work, for instances, various "autonomous" historical processes involving political, economic, and social factors. Let us first deal with gender inequality. Discussing these factors, Simi Afonja (1981) asserts that traditional customs may lead themselves, under changing conditions, to inegalitarian developments. For example, even in subsistence economies, such as the Yoruba, landownership may be limited to men and men may control women's labor and reproduction. In discussing cash crop developments and their effects on "the egalitarianism of such a precapitalist society" (p. 306), she remarks:

"the entire enterprise was initiated by Africans" (p. 310) adapting local customs to new products. She emphasizes, "The salient point to be considered in understanding the subsequent transformation to an inegalitarian structure is that men, particularly in patrilineal households, exploited their position as guardians of family and lineage values, status, and resources" (p. 306).

Regarding violence against women, such autonomous political, economic and social factors are also associated with the general level of violence. These linkages are evident in information about state societies, including Sumer, the earliest state society so far discovered. The Sumerian civilization emerged from gender-egalitarian societies such as Catal Hüyük. Moreover, in Sumer, according to Rohrlich (1980), the subjugation of women was related to militarism and the political consolidation of a patriarchal class society. Besides engaging in chronic warfare aimed at the capture of tribute, slaves, and land, the Sumerian state destroyed gender equality and democratic clan institutions wherever necessary, by violence.

On the other hand, chronic warfare alone does not necessarily affect women's status negatively. Especially when a society is being subjected to colonial wars, the effect of warfare also depends on whether other aspects of a dominating imperial culture aside from economic relations are being assimilated. One example involves the struggle by the Bari (commonly referred to as the "Motilones") of Colombia against invasions by Spanish, Colombian, and Venezuelan colonizers in the sixteenth century. The Bari are described as a fully egalitarian, gentle, classless society (Buenaventura-Posso and Brown, 1980). However, unlike other indigenous neighboring groups who were being enslaved, absorbed as workers and mercenaries, or simply decimated, the Bari continually fought back, attacking colonial landholders and successfully resisting organized military expeditions. In spite of their show of fierceness, Sabastian Joseph Guillan, a colonial envoy, noted in 1772, that this much-feared group remained internally peaceable. In the first written description of the Bari, Guillan wrote: "Between themselves one does not see fights or even heated discussions" (Buenaventura-Posso and Brown 1980, p. 121). Regarding this paradoxical situation, being at once aggressive to outsiders and harmonious within, anthropologists Elisa Buenaventura-Posso and Susan Brown (1980) state: "Two points, then, should be made clear: (1) the aggressive and hostile behavior exhibited by the Bari towards the surrounding colonizing societies was a successful self-defense reaction to threats of usurpation and extinction and (2) the harmonious, classless, internal social organization characteristic of the Bari was not altered by their fierce struggle for self-preservation" (p. 68). The authors continue:

> The first point needs little elaboration . . . the Bari have the highest regard for peace and only fight out of extreme necessity — to defend themselves from attack and to recover possessions lost at the hands of outsiders. The second point deserves fuller attention for, while the classless nature of Amazon horticultural societies has been frequently reported, such groups are not generally described as harmonious and peace-loving. In fact, studies of South American groups that have been *more extensively exposed* [our emphasis] to Western imperialism, such as the Yanömamö, the Mundurucù, and the Jivaro, indicate quite the opposite. In such societies we find reported not only hostile relations with neighbors, but also a high degree of intragroup antagonism between the genders, including such behaviors as verbal combat, the gang rape of women and woman beating (p. 114–115).

In 1964, after three centuries of efforts to "civilize" them, the Bari defenses were finally broken by a young North American missionary who originated the Motilon Development Plan. Under this plan, men are being cultivated as chiefs and given education and Colombian citizenship; patriarchal nuclear family units are replacing collective living units; wage labor for men and cash cropping are being introduced; women's work is shifting from production of fabrics, baskets and food to services such as washing clothes, and their role as healers is being usurped (Buenaventura-Posso and Brown, 1980). While the older generation of Bari still resists, a slight tendency toward cultural change is now becoming apparent among the younger Bari. According to Buenaventura-Posso and Brown (1980), "The future of those Bari groups or individuals who continue to be exposed extensively to the Western culture and economic system seems decided. Slowly, they will be absorbed into industrial society, mainly as peasants, while a few Bari males will enter into slightly more privileged positions. Today, this process is well under way and the sexual equality and individual autonomy characteristic of the Bari are already in the process of disintegration" (p. 131). It appears that, so long as the Bari were able to resist the imperial Western culture, their military engagements did not destroy their gender equality. Accomplishing this end required a deep penetration of the so-called civilized institutions into the structure and culture of the Bari society.

Consequently, we have noted (1983) that some modes of production encourage higher levels of violence involving (as economic policies) war, cattle raiding, territorial conquest, slavery and so on. On the other hand, we have also suggested that if the socioeconomic relationships within a society are not themselves conducive to violence, then this violence has to emerge from some external sources. And if these socioeconomic relationships are not conducive to gender inequality, then there have to be mechanisms based on the assimilation of external relationships that engender inequality.

Thus, to clarify the interrelations between changes in gender inequality, levels of violence and socioeconomic developments, we take note of the degree to which sexism and violence have been *imposed* on archaic societies *by outsiders* whose influence also increases the general levels of violence within these societies. Over the centuries, thousands of bands and tribes have been forced to adopt social standards that actively discriminate against women. In recent years, in addition, most of the remaining egalitarian societies have been undergoing similar transformations because of their contact with class societies. The association between gender equality and commodity relations is largely based on the impact of metropolitan class societies on precapitalist formations.

In addition to Africa and South America, such outside contacts have, also, more or less changed the highly egalitarian horticultural people of North America, including the Iroquois and Huron of the American Northwest, the Cherokee of the Southeast, and the Hopi and Zuñi of the Southwest, according to Eleanor Leacock. She asserts this claim after examining documentary evidence about the prior status of women in these societies.

Dramatic examples of outsiders imposing sexism can be found among the Montagnais-Naskapi bands. Jesuit priests, during the seventeenth century, came among these bands, backed up by military support. Arrogant about the rightness of their own convictions, they imposed European standards on both men and women. The Superior of the Jesuit Mission at Quebec, Paul Le Jeune, for instance, spent the full winter of 1633–1634 traveling in the interior with a Montagnais band. He wrote chronicles of this period, recording in them his contempt for the independence enjoyed by all band members (Leacock and Goodman, 1976). Le Jeune wrote: "As [the band members] have neither political organization, nor offices, nor dignitaries, nor any authority, for they only obey their Chief through good will toward him, therefore they never kill each other to acquire these honors. Also, as they are contented with a mere living, not one of them gives himself to the Devil to acquire wealth" (p. 80). Le Jeune felt that the establishment of political authority based on a system of permanent chiefs was essential to civilizing aboriginal peoples. Le Jeune also believed that corporal punishment would have to replace the customary forms of compensation for wrongs committed by band members. With regard to the family, attitudes of men and women had to be changed through religious training in which a man, for instance, was instructed "that he was the master and that in France women do not rule their husbands" (p. 79).

The sexual autonomy of the Montagnais was especially shocking to Le Jeune, who bemoaned the absence of patriarchy. He tells this anecdote about a discussion with a man belonging to the band: "I told him that it was not honorable for a woman to love anyone else except for her husband, and that this evil being among them, he himself was not sure that his son, who was there present, was his son. He [the Montagnais] replied, 'Thou hast no sense. You French people love only your own children; but we all love all the children of our tribe.' I began to laugh, seeing that he philosophized in horse and mule fashion" (p. 82).

Supporting such transformations in social and political life, in the Montagnais society, was the evolution of commodity relationships based on the fur trade and other commodity markets. Communal and egalitarian customs were soon undermined by a system of private property relations with its economic individualism and competition. Eventually, individual control over hunting and fur-bearing territories along with monogamy, fidelity of women, and the principle of masculine supremacy were consolidated among the Montagnais. Such changes did not completely eradicate egalitarian traditions among the band members, but they undermined these traditions and encouraged systematic warfare against other tribes competing in the fur trade.

In the preface of her book of collected articles, Leacock (1981) comments on how egalitarian social relations are undermined. She notes that in societies that are otherwise egalitarian, "indications of male dominance turn out to be due to either: (1) the effects of colonization and/or involvement in market relations . . . ; (2) the concomitant of developing inequality in a society, commonly referred to in anthropological writings as 'ranking,' when trade is encouraging specialization of labor and production for exchange is accompanying production for use . . . ; or (3) problems arising from interpretations of data in terms of western concepts or assumptions" (p. 4–5).

Furthermore, it is possible to posit that in relation to sexual inequality, modes of production that establish such rankings, and warfare that encourages masculine monopoly of organized violence, though independent, have additive effects, and that these effects *converge* in class societies. Rape, as we know, repeats itself throughout the annals of class societies. The conquering hordes of Genghis Khan raped and plundered during their innumerable forays. European feudal mercenaries, when fighting in neighboring principalities, raped women and looted towns and villages. Homecoming bands of sixteenth-century British soldiers, embittered by denial of pay and defeat abroad, raped and pillaged at will after landing on English soil. The Force Publique of the Congo, a native colonial army, adopted the ethos of their imperial Belgian masters; they too raped and plundered Congolese people. Furthermore, early accounts of the Iroquois and other American seaboard tribes indicate that rape was not used in warfare before the Europeans arrived. Tribal societies in the New World, conquered by European settlers, learned to meet force with force, adopting the new violent tactics of the conquerers along with their more sophisticated weapons. For example, the Europeans raped Indian women, burned villages, scalped the men in punitive raids, and in some cases massacred entire tribes in order to force the Indians from the land. In retaliation, rape and other tactics were used by the Indians who sought to match the Europeans' ruthlessness and ferocity. In the Philippines today these events are being partly reenacted. Coveting the traditional territories of neighboring tribal communities, Christian settlers hire thugs and bandits to rape and terrorize the tribes (Nance, 1975).

Consequently, in an endless spiral of cruelty and violent counter-reactions, numerous forms of violence, including rape, were conferred on the people of the world. Rape itself became associated with violent practices organized around broader aims: the subjugation of women and the exploitation of tribes, classes, and other social groups. Violence became the focus of a seemingly endless struggle by individuals, classes, and nations for power and property.

We have considered some mechanisms of interpersonal violence, first showing that they can include *perceivable* social pressures backed by military force. Now we will describe a social mechanism that is *hardly discernible*, because it involves circumstances in which violence seems to emerge from purely personal motives and not society at all. In other writings, we spell out the historical conditions that have concentrated men in commodity production outside the home, and women in household activities. These conditions have encouraged customary practices that vest family authority in husbands and define housewives as personal dependents so long as the housewife is dependent on her husband's wage to purchase commodities. Even though this relationship between commodity ownership, status, and authority may not be reflected in some of the newer laws about married women's rights, its influence still pervades everyday life. (Rosoff and Tobach, 1978–1985.) Also, because of these restrictions and dominant moral standards in capitalist societies, the dependency of women has been equated ideologically with inferior abilities and capacities. Such ideological equations also enter into the determination of the status relations that legitimate sexual inequality.

Similar changes in family economies, dominant-submissive relations, and violence against wives continue to occur today in developing nations. A study by Patricia Draper (1975) dealing with the impact of modern African labor markets on village family relationships illustrates these changes. Although they are taking place under different circumstances, the effects of capitalism on sexual relations and patriarchal violence, in this study, parallel the changes that occurred in Western societies. Draper's study of a single tribe is also significant because it contrasts aboriginal !Kung *band* sexual equality and relatively nonviolent family relations, on the one hand, with !Kung *village* inequality and greater family violence, on the other.

Draper's field experiences focus on the !Kung Bushmen aboriginal bands that forage on the edges of the great Kalahari Desert. However, in addition, she details the changing patterns of life among those band members who have migrated into village settlements. In the villages the egalitarianism of the band is disappearing, yet this change does not appear to be imposed by any physical force from the outside. Importantly, from the standpoint of everyday life, it seems to arise *spontaneously* from the personal inclinations and the changing roles and relationships of people inside the village itself.

Draper's (1975) observations being with the familiar correspondence between primitive communism and gender equality. She notes that among the people living in bands, in the economic sphere, which is based on hunting and gathering, !Kung women have personal autonomy. Also, there is no rigid sextyping for most adult activities, including domestic chores and raising children in their communal society. Finally, the !Kung nomads are gentle and actively discourage any sign of harmful competition among males and violence between the sexes. The aboriginal bands are unquestionably characterized by gender equality,

All of this is changing, however, as the !Kung are relocating in villages where the economy is partly organized around commodity production. This commodity activity involves the private ownership of livestock on land surrounding a village and the exploitation of masculine wage labor in nearby Bantu or European settlements (Draper, 1975). In the villages, the authority of men is gradually increasing and the status of women is declining.

Why are these changes taking place? Partly it is because the desire for higher living standards encourages the men to leave the village, frequently for several days at a time, to work for Bantu employers. When they return, their authority is heightened by their control over goat and cattle raising and their mastery of the Bantu language and customs. These work experiences and the knowledge of Bantu also encourage patricipation by men. In political relations that are largely based on contacts with the other settlements.

Village women likewise have become enmeshed in household economies whose material inventory is much richer than that of the nomadic bands. In the village, food preparation becomes more complicated. Furthermore, Draper (1975) says, "Women do the greatest part of the cooking, and they also do most of the [food] drying and storing" (p. 101). Household possessions also require more energy to maintain. The women, therefore, spend more time and work harder at domestic tasks.

In addition, village relations are being affected by severe economic and political constraints that operate behind the scenes. The village economy is organized around independent peasant households, and it is essentially based on a precapitalist mode of production in the process of being shaped by its articulation with a capitalist mode of production. However — unlike the Montagnais under seventeenth-century French colonial rule — there is no military or religious institution blatantly imposing these changes in the village itself. Instead, the allocation of men, in everyday life, to commodity production and women to household labor, outside of the economic constraints, appears to be based on spontaneous choices exercised freely by individuals.

Along with their competition for status and material wealth, the men are becoming more aggressive and contemptuous of women. In the nomadic bands, a woman finding herself with an uncongenial husband quickly leaves his company and spends a year or two in casual flirtations before marrying again. In the village, however, couples are held together in fitful marriages by economic pressures. At the same time, public censure is addressed to the wife; and slander by boastful husbands in public settings deflects social criticism of marital conflicts away from the men (Draper, 1975).

Simultaneously, the organization of space and privacy in the villages isolates marital conflicts. Village men spend more of their time in economic activities away from the village or on its periphery while women are more restricted to the household economy centered on the residence. Moreover, in the bush, choice of residence is such that over time married couples live about equally — often simultaneously — with the kin of both the husband and wife. Consequently, a bushwoman who is involved in a marital dispute usually has several of her kin to support her interests nearby. Village wives, however, live only with their husbands and are more readily denied such support because the family is considered a private sphere. "In the bush," Draper (1975) says, "people can see each other and determine, on a variety of grounds, whether it is appropriate or timely to initiate social interaction. In the . . . villages one heard such exchanges as 'So-and-so, are you at home?' and 'Shall I enter [your space]?'" (p. 107–108).

These apparently spontaneous developments are also creating new patterns of violence among the men. After experiencing the gentleness of the nomadic bands and the joyful camaraderie shared by both sexes, Draper (1975) was chilled when she heard a !Kung woman say: "If a [village] man is angry with his wife he could put her in their house, bolt the door and beat her. No one could get in to separate them. They could only hear her screams" (p. 109). The same !Kung woman observed that this violence would not occur among the people in her nomadic band.

THE POLITICS OF SOCIOBIOLOGY

As indicated, some of the major alternatives to sociobiological theories of rape have been influenced by feminist theories. In this section we show that feminist and sociobiological perspectives provide different conceptions of feminine behavior as well as alternative approaches to rape prevention.

Feminist theories point to wide variations in gender relationships, while sociobiological theories take a narrow androcentric view. Victim-precipitation theories provide flagrant examples of this androcentric bias because they assume victims are to blame—that victims instigate the assault. Compared with Menachim Amir's (1971) conventional non-biological theory which claimed that seductive behavior by women encouraged rape, the sociobiologists, Shields and Shields, find victim precipitation in the mere physical presence of vulnerable women. Women who do not allow men to have their way precipitate their own rape. Even women who discriminate against any man or class of men, precipitate rape. According to Shields and Shields (1983; 115–23), "The external stimulus for rape is a sufficiently vulnerable female . . . . Perception of an unwilling female is almost invariably a part of the stimulus controlling rape . . . .If any female discriminates against *any* male (or class of males), while the male is morphologically and physiologically capable of *forcing* copulation with little or no risk to himself (e.g., because he is significantly larger or possesses superior weapons), and if the act has even a small probability of successful fertilization, then selection may favor a forcible rape tactic." For an analysis of traditional victim-precipitation ideas, see Schwendinger and Schwendinger (1974) and Denmark and Friedman's article on rape myths in the monograph.

Feminists criticize traditional social science theories that attribute gender inequality to inherent masculine aggressiveness and feminine passivity. Elsewhere, we (1976) critique rape theories with similar standpoints. We now find that sociobiologists have added their own contributions to this androcentric genre. Thornhill and Thornhill (1983) assert that females, in contrast to males throughout the world, are passive and afraid of taking risks. According to these authors, "sexual competition seems greater among males than among females in humans throughout the world . . . human males will have evolved to employ a higher-risk, higher-stake strategy than females" (p. 148).

Thus, in addition, it is the canny male who "is expected to shift from alternatives of lower reproductive return to alternatives of higher reproductive return depending on available opportunities" (p. 164). It is the human male, not the female, who upon reaching adulthood is faced with risky reproductive alternatives. One of these alternatives is rape if the male lacks the resources to gain mates for reproduction any other way. In this androcentric view, women are mere receptacles as men compete with each other to "place ejaculate in the female's reproductive tract."

We have said that feminist and sociobiological perspectives represent alternative approaches to rape prevention. Feminist alternatives do not ignore punishment as a deterrence for rape or other forms of violence against women. However, the weight of their alternatives rests on broader social policies. Sociobiologists, on the other hand, are silent about broader policies and sharply concentrate on severe punishments.

The sociobiologists are continuous with their ideological forefathers. The lack of interest in broader social policies also characterized the 19th century social Darwinists. For instance, Malthus believed that government supports would not deter immorality among the poor. His theory, in fact, implied that broader policies would make matters worse. As indicated, he said that the poor were morally responsible for their own misery by having more children than they could afford, and that they would continue to propagate and create a greater imbalance in the population-food ratio if they were aided by "poor law" legislation. Malthus' theory provided the outstanding rationale against out-of-door [home] relief programs. The eventual destruction of these programs, especially in the agrarian sector, made available huge numbers of unemployed and starving workers for industrial labor markets.

Spencer, too, felt that the government had few positive functions besides policing citizens, controlling fires, and providing military defense. He vehemently opposed public education, social security legislation, public health programs, and other welfare-state policies because he said they enabled "inferior" people to survive. Spencer, not Darwin, created the phrase, "survival of the fittest," and he believed that laissez-faire capitalism and its "free market" enabled the fittest to survive. If competitive industrial forces were not checked by government policies, he believed that white Anglo-Saxon and Teutonic "races" would eventually consolidate their superior position and dominate the earth. In this process, inferior individuals and "races" would die out. The human species would only be composed of the most highly evolved beings, and it would compete more effectively with other species for survival.

Both Malthusian and social Darwinian ideas still have currency today among some intellectuals. But their biological reasoning is derived from class and racial myths rather than scientific explanations. Malthus' mathematical estimates of growth rates, in population and food supplies, were not based on empirical reality. Demographic research indicates that population growth has little to do with the "impulse for propagation" created by natural selection. High infant mortality rates and precarious economic conditions, especially in agrarian societies, produce a need for high birth rates. Low birth rates characterize highly industrialized countries where infant mortality is low, individual welfare is less dependent on family size, and elders are primarily supported by social security nets rather than their children. Finally, epidemics, famines, crimes, war, poverty, occupational deaths, and so forth are no longer significant factors limiting population growth. The human species does not stand helpless in the face of so-called natural forces. The study of human evolution reveals an ever increasing capacity to control the birth rate and to manipulate, change and expand food supplies. This capacity has enveloped the entire planet with interdependent economic systems. Today, famine in any part of the world cannot be attributed to natural regional conditions such as drought. The great famine in North Africa, for instance, is created by economic and political relations that have produced the massive erosion of arable land, the class and imperial factors that control the distribution of food within nation-states, and the maldistribution of economic resources that maintains the differences between highly developed imperial nations and third-world economies.

The biological theories of crime influenced by Spencer also lack credibility. Criminals are not biologically inferior beings and their antisocial behavior can be prevented by broader social policies, not only by fear of punishment.

Given the limits of the sociobiological perspective, it is not surprising to find little mention of crime prevention policies. Shields and Shields (1983) concentrate their recommendations entirely on conservative "law-and-order" solutions. Retribution and severe punishments are regarded as the most important means for deterring rape. It is suggested that rape would be reduced to a minimum if "the probability and severity of retribution were maximized" (p. 133). These sociobiologists are so committed to swift, sure and severe punishment that they claim it would deter rape whether or not their theory of rape is correct. Almost as an afterthought, they note that overcrowding in urban wastelands, poverty and unequal opportunity may encourage rape. But rather than forthrightly attacking these social problems, they promote moral indignation. They "predict that when a society regards the rape of *any* woman the way individuals perceive the rape of their daughters, sisters or mates, and then resists, pursues, and punishes the rapists accordingly, rape will cease to be a major problem" (p. 133).

Let us now describe some broader social policies aimed at rape prevention. It should be kept in mind, however, that our previous discussion of research influenced by feminist developments emphasized anthropological studies. It did not detail research on industrial countries. Research in such countries has focused on rape of non-wives, rape in marriage, sexual harassment, abuse of children and so forth. It has examined cultural standards, supremist ideologies, individual attitudes and social learning processes. To further understand violence against women, there have also been studies of the mass media, violent pornography and community relationships. An explosion of new information on violence especially within the United States has appeared within the last decade.

As a result, writings influenced by feminist developments have, with a few exceptions, encouraged a more scientifically grounded approach to crime prevention. (For discussion of the exceptions, see Edwards, 1976; and Schwendinger and Schwendinger, 1976.) In regard to certain types of rapes, researchers have repeatedly shown the importance of the same racial and social class relationships that affect other violent crimes, such as ordinary assault and robbery (Schwendinger and Schwendinger, 1983). They also provide evidence that the prevention of rape in the United States is significantly tied to the prevention of most "street crimes." Consequently, social policies must be aimed at changing the conditions that generate higher incidences of direct interpersonal violence among marginal members of the labor force as well as among men whose livelihoods are at least partly based on illegal activities such as robbery. Sexual assaults by strangers and other non-family members, that is, rape as "street crime," can be reduced enormously by changing the conditions of life in poorer working-class communities.

Antirape groups have rightfully insisted that rapists should receive swift and certain punishment; and they have proposed policies concerning the apprehension, conviction and punishment of these criminals. Today, however, people must avoid the seduction of simpleminded law-and-order policies that deceptively promise far more than they can deliver, especially without broader social changes. In contrast, there is a solid body of evidence that relates "street crimes" to social and economic conditions. There is also evidence that public policies can decrease unemployment, substandard housing for the poor and deterioration of working-class communities through urban planning and the expansion of public-sector jobs in such areas as mass transportation, community development, housing and health care.

In addition, it should be kept in mind that rape and sexual extortion are committed by middle- and upper-class males and known assailants, such as employers, work superiors, husbands and other family members. There is a high incidence of sexual violence in wartime among men from *all* classes, especially when these men are infused with racial and national chauvinisms. Since personal dependency relations, workplace subordination and chauvinistic standards are causally significant, the reduction of sexual violence requires a variety of measures. Such measures include meaningful non-discriminatory full employment legislation to generate jobs for women as well as men; legislative and trade union reforms that enhance the power and status of women in the workplace; militant activity that opposes the use of sexist stereotypes by commercial establishments especially when those stereotypes are combined with violence; and passing laws that prohibit rape in marriage and that make divorce an inexpensive and feasible alternative for abused wives. The passage of the Equal Rights Amendment would certainly be a positive force in this context.

The reduction of the dependency of women at home and in the labor market is extremely important because it provides individual women with the power to dictate the basic terms on which men must relate to them. In this connection, Diana Russell's (1982) research found that wives who were primary breadwinners when their husbands first raped them were more likely to take effective action. Her study further showed that 100 percent of the wives who were providing the total family income when they were fiirst raped were no longer married to their rapist husbands. Economic independence and workplace experience give wives greater strength to assert their own rights against abusive men. Wives who are dependent tend to remain in violent family relationships. Also, research by Pauline Bart and Patricia O'Brien (1980) and others would suggest that assertiveness training can often help prevent rape inside or outside of family relationships, whether or not women are economically independent.

Sexist stereotypes also need special attention because sexual aggression, and aggression in general, are socially learned rather than biologically determined behavior. How, then, can society stop *teaching* men to rape? Reducing the patterns of violence that can be acquired through direct experience and reducing the models for such violence provided in the home, by the mass media, and by other commercial establishments would be helpful. For example, Bandura (1973) indicated that exposure to televised violence promoted aggressiveness in children. Other research indicates that influential models for violent behavior are found in the home (intrafamilial aggression or parents explicitly teaching children to use violence outside the home), among peers, and in the media. (Schwendinger and Schwendinger, 1985.)

The mass media are extremely important because they provide models for children's behavior. Sexual aggression on the screen either must be replaced, or, at least must be identified with negative consequences that reinforce proper moral attitudes and that cultivate an unambiguous sense of aversion to sexual violence (Bandura, 1973). A number of individual feminists and women's groups have focused on this issue. However, strategies for change in this area would be helped enormously by the development of guidelines for political action that distinguish between erotic symbolism that has no effect on sexual violence and symbolism, such as sadomasochistic pornography, that has such an effect. Feshbach (1978), concludes that the depiction of violence in pornography can have decided negative effects. Recent studies by Feshbach and Malamuth (1980) suggest that males, in particular, are prone to use violent erotica to reinterpret expressions of pain on the part of female rape victims as indications of sexual excitement. On the other hand, these guidelines must not conflict with the First Amendment (the "free speech" amendment) to the Constitution, or in the long run, especially given the conservative mood in the United States, they will do more harm than good. The development of such guidelines should be informed by research that distinguishes the effects of different kinds of sexual symbolism on individual behavior. Erotic symbolism per se does not encourage sexual violence (Bandura, 1973). Pornographic presentations that depict the violent victimization of women do reinforce violent behavior positively (Feshbach, 1978; Feshbach and Malamuth, 1980).

Measures for reducing the cultivation of violence among children are implicated in any policy that increases the power of wives to determine their relations with husbands. However, such efforts as Family Anonymous and women's shelters for battered women are also important in this context. Avenues emphasizing prevention would include educational courses in parenting for high school students and/or couples planning to have children. These programs could emphasize the profound effects that family violence has on children. The government should support the development of educational research and programs that combat family violence through education and the mass media.

Finally, the prevention of violence against women should be vitally concerned with the incredible horror inflicted on women in war (Creel, 1944; Brownmiller, 1975; Roy, 1975; Schwendinger and Schwendinger, 1983). This prevention requires political opposition to militaristic government policies that reinforce the general level of violence at home and abroad. Such policies escalate violence against women enormously by supporting military dictatorships abroad and by fostering a worldwide arms race leading to new wars. No one single approach — neither penal punishment nor assertiveness training for women — is sufficient. What is needed to prevent rape, is a full scale combined approach including the broader elements mentioned above.

REFERENCES

Afonja, Simi. (1981). Changing modes of production and the sexual division of labor among the Yoruba. *Signs, 7,* 299–313.

Amir, Menachem. (1971). *Patterns in forcible rape.* Chicago: University of Chicago Press.

Ardrey, Robert. (1966). *Territorial imperative.* New York: Dell Publishers.

Bandura, Albert. (1973). *Aggression: A social learning analysis.* Englewood Cliffs: Prentice Hall.

Bart, Pauline, B. and O'Brien, Patricia, (1980). How to say no to Storaska and survive: Rape avoidance strategies. Paper presented at the Annual Meeting of the American Sociological Association, New York.

Brownmiller, Susan. (1975). *Against our will: Men, women and rape.* New York: Simon and Schuster.

Buenaventura-Posso, Elisa and Brown, Susan E. (1980). Forced transition from egalitarianism to male dominance: The Bari of Colombia. In Mona Etienne and Eleanor Leacock (Eds.), *Women and colonization* (pp. 109–133). New York: Praeger.

Caulfield, Mina Davis. (1977). Universal sex oppression? — A critique from Marxist anthropology. *Catalyst, 10/11*, 60–77.

Clark, Lorenne M. G. and Lewis, Debra J. (1977). *Rape: The price of coercive sexuality.* Toronto: Women's Education Press.

Creel, George, (1944). *War criminals and punishment.* New York: R. M. McBridge and Co.

Diamond, Stanley, (1971). The rule of law versus the order of custom. *Social Research, 38*, 42–72.

Draper, Patricia, (1975). !Kung women: Contrasts in sexual egalitarianism in foraging and sedentary contexts. In Rayna R. Reiter (Ed.), *Toward an anthropology of women* (pp. 77–109). New York: Monthly Review Press.

Edwards, Allison. (1976). *Rape, racism, and the white women's movement: An answer to Susan Brownmiller.* Chicago: Sojourner Truth Organization.

Estioko-Griffin, Agnes and Griffin, P. Bion. (1981). Woman the hunter: The Agta. In Frances Dahlberg (Ed.), *Woman the gatherer.* New Haven, CT: Yale University Press.

Feshbach, Seymour. (1980, August 3). Mixing sex with violence — A dangerous alchemy. *New York Times*, section 2

Feshbach, Seymour and Malamuth, Neal. (1978, November). Sex and aggression: Proving the link. *Psychology Today, 12*, pp. 110–114, 116–117, 122.

Hofstadter, R. (1959). *Social Darwinism in American thought.* New York: George Braziller.

Leacock, Eleanor Burke. (1975). Introduction. In Frederick Engels, *The origin of the family, private property and the state* (pp. 7–67). New York: International.

Leacock, Eleanor Burke. (1981). *Myths of male dominance, collected articles on women cross-culturally.* New York: Monthly Review Press.

Leacock, Eleanor and Goodman, Jacqueline. (1976). Montagnais marriage and the Jesuits in the seventeenth century: Incidents from the relations of Paul Le Jeune. *Western Canadian Journal of Anthropology, 6*, 77–91.

Lorenz, Konrad, (1966). *On aggression.* New York: Harcourt, Brace and World.

Malthus, Thomas P. (1914). *An essay on population*, I. New York: E. P. Dutton. (Originally published in 1798).

Mead, Margaret. (1963). *Sex and temperament.* New York: Dell.

Nance, John (1975). *The gentle Tasaday.* New York: Harcourt Brace Jovanovich.

Rohrlich, Ruby. (1980). State formation in Sumer and the subjugation of women. *Feminist Studies, 6*, 76–102.

Rohrlich-Leavitt, Ruby, Sykes, Barbara, and Weatherford, Elizabeth. (1975). Aboriginal woman: Male and female anthropological perspectives. In Rayna R. Reiter (Ed.), *Toward an anthropology of women* (pp. 110–126). New York: Monthly Review Press.

Rosoff, Betty and Tobach, Ethel. (1978–1985). *Genes and gender series*. New York: Gordian Press.

Roy, K. K. (1975). Feelings and attitudes of raped woman of Bangladesh towards military personnel of Pakistan. In Israel Drapkin and Emilio Viano (Eds.), *Victimology: A new focus*, Vol. 5 (pp. 65–72), Lexington, MA: D. C. Heath and Co.

Russell, Diana E. H. (1982). *Rape in marriage*. New York: Macmillan.

Sacks, Karen. (1975). Engels revisited: Women, the organization of production, and private property. In Rayna R. Reiter (Ed.), *Toward an anthropology of women* (pp. 211–234), New York: Monthly Review Press.

Sanday, Peggy R. (1981). The socio-cultural context of rape: A cross-cultural study. *Journal of Social Issues, 37*, 5–27.

Schwendinger, Herman and Schwendinger, Julia. (1985). *Adolescent subcultures and delinquency*, New York: Praeger.

Schwendinger, Julia and Schwendinger, Herman. (1974). Rape myths: In legal, theoretical and everyday practice. *Crime and Social Justice, 13*, 18–26.

Schwendinger, Julia and Schwendinger, Herman. (1976). A review of the rape literature. *Crime and Social Justice, 6*, 79–85.

Schwendinger, Julia and Schwendinger, Herman. (1983). *Rape and inequality*. Beverly Hills, CA: Sage Publishers.

Shields, William, M. and Shields, Lea M. (1983). Forcible rape: An evolutionary perspective. *Ethology and Sociobiology, 4*, 115–136.

Spencer, Herbert. (1852). A theory of population, deduced from the general law of animal fertility. *The Westminster Review, 1*, 468–501.

Thornhill, Randy and Thornhill, Nancy W. (1983). Human rape: An evolutionary analysis. *Ethology and Sociobiology, 4*, 137–173.

Turnbull, Colin. (1981). Mbuti womanhood. In Frances Dahlberg (Ed.), *Woman the gatherer* (pp. 205–219). New Haven, CT: Yale University Press.

THE LANGUAGE OF SEXUAL VIOLENCE: MORE THAN A MATTER OF SEMANTICS

Julie Blackman
BARNARD COLLEGE

> At any rate when a subject is highly
> controversial . . . one can not hope to tell
> the truth. One can only show how one came to
> hold the opinion one does hold. One can only
> give one's audience the chance of drawing
> their own conclusions as they observe the
> limitations, the prejudices, the
> idiosyncracies of the speaker.
>
> VIRGINIA WOOLF

This chapter is primarily concerned with the controversy that surrounds the use of the word *rape* as a legitimate and appropriate description of apparently forced copulation in non-human species. The debate over the choice of this word has been made especially heated by the disturbing tendency for sociobiologists not only to apply the word *rape* to non-humans, but also to argue that rape is of evolutionary and reproductive value. (See Baron, 1984, for a critique of such sociobiological theories of rape.) In justifying this choice of scientific terminology, sociobiologists have provided a positively valued context for rape. (Hagen, 1979; Shields and Shields, 1983; Thiessen, 1983; Thornhill and Thornhill, 1983). Such an affirmative, Darwinian-derived construction of *rape* undermines feminist definitions of rape as an aggressive act, that is neither sexual nor reproductively useful.

This chapter, then, was written, first, to address these questions: Why use the word *rape* to describe apparently forced copulation in non-human species, and why define it in terms which assign it evolutionary significance? Also, a consideration of what *rape* means to a woman who has experienced it, and a discussion of the nature of treatment for rape survivors are included.

LINGUISTIC CHOICES: WHY ARE SOCIOBIOLOGISTS TALKING ABOUT RAPE?

The idea that language conveys meaning is so obvious that it would scarcely bear mentioning, were it not for the fact that the use of language — the choice of words — regularly involves more than a simple selection of some available descriptor. Language users make word choices that are based upon such factors as their level of affect, their beliefs about the listener's attitudes about the topic being discussed, the desired impact, and so on. Thus, the diversity and versatility of language provide speakers with word choices for the same object or event that may be formal or informal, colorful or bland, evocative or superficial. Further, while "normal speech" may be more spontaneous than planned, prepared text can be assumed, by its very nature, to involve the author in a word choice process carefully designed to enhance intended impact.

Some words are more connotatively powerful than others. Some words reflect values that are deeply held and firmly enmeshed in systems of associations, whereas others address less central concerns. Further, words which pertain to interpersonal, relational events are especially likely to reflect prevailing cultural norms. As norms about interpersonal events change, so do the meanings associated with the words that denote and connote these events. For example, the October 9, 1984 issue of *Time* magazine featured a story entitled, "Sex in the 80's: The Revolution is Over." Contained within the article was a subsection, "Saying What You Mean." The author of this mini-dictionary wrote an introductory explanation about the need for updated definitions of actions relevant to sexual behavior: "The language of love has always been a series of coded signals, sometimes hard to read, sometimes easy, often deceptive, always changing." Adjectives like "sensitive" and "strong" are defined. We learn, for example, that "sensitive" is a "term of praise when applied to men. Stereotypical, and thus insensitive, when applied to women;" while "strong" is a term of praise when applied to women. When applied to men, it implies a tendency toward insensitivity, even machismo." Thus do the mass media shape and perhaps reflect changing cultural norms.

Within the presumably more linguistically demanding scientific community, language is an issue with both methodological and substantive implications. Clarity and precision of language are necessary for replicability and for the accurate dissemination of one's findings. However, when the topics under investigation are relational and value-laden, word choices take on additional dimensions of importance. Clearly, the primary concern, here, with regard to linguistic impact, pertains to the choice of the word *rape* to convey meaning about forced copulatory activity in such species as elephant seals, scorpion flies, mallards, green-winged teals, bank swallows, magpies, frogs, snow geese, worms, bedbugs, orangutans, and a variety of fish. (See Harding's chapter for the references associated with the preceding list.) One must ask about the intentions of the word choosers and their anticipated impact. Why would ostensibly objective scientists appear to overlook the certain cognitive and affective associations that accompany *rape*? Whose interests are served by deliberately de-politicizing rape and applying this word to non-human species?

It should be noted that extensive attention to these questions creates a paradox — as one discusses them, the selection decisions that led sociobiologists to choose the word *rape* are legitimized. In addition, the ultimate point that the word *rape* should simply not be used when discussing non-human species is a simple one. Thus, one fears going beyond "beating a dead horse," into the realm of "beating a rocking horse." That is, one risks dealing at length with word choices that are not only "senseless," but that may have been without "senses" to begin with. Nonetheless, with attendant risks acknowledged, these questions are addressed.

Certainly, emphasis on evolutionarily beneficial consequences of rape antagonizes the collective social conscience that has emerged in the wake of feminist attention to sexual violence. See, for example, the October, 1983 issue of the *American Psychological Association Monitor* for a description of feminists' reactions to the title of Thiessen's (1983) paper which depicted rape as a "reproductive strategy," and "our evolutionary legacy." There, Thiessen responded to criticisms of the title by saying, "The title says what I wanted it to say. There are reproductive and evolutionary implications to rape" (p. 22).

Consider that sociobiologists who advance biological explanations for social characteristics would support the notion that patriarchies exist in human societies as the necessary result of biological imperatives, and are adaptive for the species. Feminist political thought is diametrically opposed to this "biology is appropriate destiny" view. Further, feminism has focused critical attention on the ways in which scientific activity may serve as a reactionary force deterring efforts to being about social change (Firestone, 1971; Shields, 1975). To use the word *rape* in a de-politicized context functions to undermine ten years of feminist consciousness-raising. It would seem only to serve the interests of those who would detract from the legitimacy and seriousness of problems that have maintained women in positions of political and personal inferiority in relation to men.

SCIENCE AND THE HOPE OF OBJECTIVITY

It has been suggested, by Shields (1975), that for all of its apparent objectivity, "science plays hand-maiden to values." This acknowledgement of the potential subjectivity of science notwithstanding, scientific endeavors are imbued with special importance during this technological era, in which the rate of acquisition of knowledge charted over time explodes in logarithmic asymptotes that defy individual learning capacities. Social scientists, then, engaged in the systematic study of social issues may find themselves in positions of high visibility, both within and outside their perceived collegial community, as they ride the crest of the science surge.

It is this coming together of the study of value-related interpersonal events — like rape — and the seriousness and the objectivity ascribed to scientific activity that creates the potential for social scientists to function as highly effective propagandizers. Further, with the advent of the women's movement, many feminist researchers have expended considerable effort in order to make their own values explicit. This process of making one's ideologies overt was often mistaken for a lack of scientific rigor among those who perceived traditional, sexist ideology as objective. Indeed, non-conscious, covert ideology, held in the absence of perceived alternatives, may feel like objectivity. Or, as Bleier (1984) wrote, "Objectivity, the ostensibly non-involved stance, is the male epistemological stance, which 'does not comprehend its own perspectivity' (MacKinnon, 1982, p. 538)." (p. 152). Deviations, then, are experienced as signs of subjectivity, rather than as indications of an alternative, equally objective ideology. Making new ideologies explicit is a complicated process, since it necessarily responds to existing, often oppositional, views. Therefore, it involves word re-definition as new perspectives are applied to old problems.

Rape: Redefined by the feminist, scientific community. Rape is an old problem that has received new attention in this country, within and outside the scientific community — particularly in the ten years that have passed since the publication of Brownmiller's (1975) *Against Our Will: Men, Women and Rape.* Rape — an act whose representation historically, in legal statutes, reflected the notion that men needed protection from vindictive women making false accusations (Berger, 1977). Rape — an act that, until recently, was legally impossible in marriage in every state. Today, it remains legally impossible in over 30 states. Rape — a word that has denoted not only an act of sexual violence, but also connoted a sense of shame and stigmatization for the girl or woman who experienced such an assault. The causal role of the rapist's intentions received less attention in cultural mythology and in social scientific investigations than the victim's susceptibility to and potential culpability for such a violation.

It is interesting to note that women who tend, more than men, to conform to the patterns of standard language usage, may circumvent a full realization of their victimization through careful linguistic construction and the avoidance of "harsh" words. For example, psychologists and sociologists who study what *they* call "marital rape" do not ask, "Has you husband ever raped you?" to identify marital rape victims. Instead, these researchers may ask, "Has your husband ever used violence or the threat of violence to force you to have sexual intercourse?" This lengthier second version was not designed for scientific precision, but because data-gathering demonstrated that the same women who said "No" to the question containing the word *rape* said "Yes" to its definitional counterpart. This difference in response tendencies indicates that admitting the occurrence of violently coerced intercourse carries less connotative weight than acknowledging that one has been *raped* by one's husband.

Joan (not her real name) provides an example of the impact of "re-naming." Joan is a 35 year-old woman who was indicted for stabbing her husband. During her efforts to explain why this had occurred, Joan described a time when her husband had solicited a stranger — a man walking by their car — for the purpose of having sexual intercourse with her. It was late, a night in winter. Joan's husband told her to take her blouse off. She tried to refuse, but he pulled a gun from his jacket pocket and demanded that she remove her clothing. He then beckoned to a male passerby and asked him if he "wanted any." This man responded that he had no money, but Joan's husband reassured him that it was free. Joan's husband told her to get into the back seat and he watched while the man had intercourse with his wife. This experience was Joan's first sexual contact with a man other than her husband. Afterward, Joan's husband told the man that he had better not tell anyone what had happened, or he would come back and find him. Joan and her husband went home. She desperately wanted to bathe, but her husband insisted that she have intercourse with him first. The next day, Joan took 11 showers.

The importance of language: Author's note. I have been careful in my retelling of Joan's story. I referred to the actions of the stranger, and subsequently, those of her husband as "intercourse." Joan referred to them as "making love." She reported this experience with a remarkable lack of affect. When she was done, I asked her if she felt she had been "raped." Then, she began to cry and said, "Yes, I was raped. That man I had never even seen before had sex with me. He raped me." She never identified her husband's "love-making" that night as "rape," although she had not wanted to have sex with him, and had pleaded to be allowed to bathe.

Applying the word *rape* to Joan's experience magnified her upset at relating what had happened. To refer to the sexual assault as "making love" redefined the actions in a way that enabled her to feel that the experience was not unique or out of the realm of her normal experience. She had "made love" before. However, the anger generated by this violation never left her, and several months later, when she stabbed her sleeping husband, her explanations for why she had acted as she did included her description of what her husband had done to her — with the aid of a stranger — on that winter's night.

Rape is a word that connotes an extreme violation of self. Describing an act of rape as "making love" functions not only to euphemize the event, but to privatize it. Making love reflects a private, consensual choice; rape is an injustice, a crime and a frightening symbol of men's domination of women in a patriarchal culture. Because of the way Joan defined what had been done to her, it never occurred to her to seek help, or to attempt to press charges against the stranger-rapist or against her husband for his actions before, during or after that rape.

TREATMENT ISSUES
FOR RAPE SURVIVORS

Joan's word choices privatized her experience, thereby preventing her from realizing that social services were available or that the criminal justice system would be interested in Joan's "personal problem." As a rape survivor, Joan was, in some senses, victimized by her commitment to making the political personal — the opposite of what feminists would have rape survivors do. Still, in other senses, Joan's redefinition enabled her to cope with what had been done to her — at least for a while.

Once a rape is "realized" and named, it is important for women to know that treatment is available, and in the remainder of this section, treatment options are detailed.

TREATMENT MODALITIES

In general, there are three kinds of psychological treatment offered to survivors of traumatic life events: (1) crisis intervention counseling, (2) follow-up care on an individual basis, and (3) follow-up care for groups. Here, the ways in which these treatment modalities might impact differentially upon different survivors with a range of self-defined rape experiences are explored. The current state of research in this area mandates that more questions will be raised than answered.

A key issue that emerged very early in considerations of counseling for rape survivors pertained to the relationship between their characteristics and those of the rapist. As will become clear, the underlying concern can be summarized with this general question: How can one best ensure that the rape survivor and the treatment provider will "speak the same language?"

A variety of more specific questions has been raised. For example, is it useful to match client and therapist on social and characterological variables? Most researchers working with rape victims agree that the rape counselor should be a woman (Schuker, 1979; Silverman, 1977). It is suggested that the presence of a man who is the counselor might traumatize the victim further. In addition, it is typically assumed that a women would be more sympathetic and understanding because she is assumed to be more likely than a man to have gone through some sort of a victimization experience herself (Schuker, 1979). (There are men who are rape victims who seek treatment, and there are men who are counselors. In general, though, it seems that victims who are men prefer to be treated by women counselors, perhaps because their victimizer was a man.)

And, should the race and/or ethnicity of the counselor and the survivor be matched? Clinicians are increasingly coming to believe that the race and/or ethnicity of the counselor and the client should be matched as well, or at least that the counselor, who is often white, should make a special effort (through training, self-awareness, etc.) to understand the minority client's position (Corkhuff and Pierce, 1967; Mizio, 1972; Vontress, 1971). It is essential that the client feel at ease with the therapist so that rapport can be established (Vontress, 1971). In general, it has been found that clients relate best to those with whom they can identify (Vontress, 1971). This is not likely to occur if the therapist is white and the client black, or some other ethnic minority, unless a special effort is made by the counselor. To the extent that such variables as race or ethnicity enhance client-therapist identification and/or affect the way in which rape is experienced or defined, a match on these traits might be advisable.

Further, should the rape counselor be a professional or a trained peer? Feminists, especially grass roots activists, have suggested that rape survivors need a sympathetic listener, and that the use of professional personnel (e.g., psychiatrist and other mental health workers) may promote the feeling in the victim that she is mentally ill (Katz and Mazur, 1979; Schuker, 1979). Alternatively, others feel that professionally trained personnel are required if adequate treatment is to be provided — if all relevant implications of the rape are to be understood (Abarbanel, 1976; Peters et al., 1976; Williams and Williams, 1973). The conclusion reached by the Center for Women's Policy Studies (Brodyaga et al., 1975) is that a combination of both professional and non-professional care should be provided. It seems reasonable to suggest that a woman who had previously been in psychotherapy and had had a positive experience would prefer a professional therapist, whereas a woman who was unfamiliar with psychotherapy and/or came from a cultural background in which the recipients of such treatment were devalued would prefer a peer counselor.

CRISIS INTERVENTION COUNSELING

While the presence of some therapist is "constant" across treatment modalities, what she/he does and the effectiveness with which she/he does it can be assumed to vary greatly. Of the three treatment modalities mentioned at the outset, crisis counseling is by far the most widely offered service. Hotlines and telephone counseling are available through community agencies (e.g., NYWAR, NOW), or, as in New York City, the Police Department (Sex Crime Analysis Unit). Counseling by telephone usually involves giving emotional support and practical advice and making appropriate referrals. Face-to-face counseling is typically provided by peer rape crisis counselors who provide immediate, non-judgmental aid and support to the survivor during the acute phase of the trauma. Generally, crisis intervention counseling takes place in the emergency room of a hospital or at the site of a community agency to which the survivor has come for care. It seems likely that immediate crisis care is an essential part of the ideal treatment for rape survivors. Rape survivors have undergone a trauma similar in scope to that of other stressful life events (e.g., severe illness or injury; loss of a loved one); support that responds to their understanding of what they have experienced will be helpful. It is suggested, therefore, that in relation to treatment recipients, survivors of rape who do not receive some sort of crisis-time psychological support — from professional counselors, non-professional advocates, family members or friends — are likely to experience traumatic consequences that are more severe, more debilitating and longer lasting (Bard, 1976); Schuker, 1979).

Still, this advocacy for treatment does not make explicit bases for matching the client with a crisis-intervention strategy. General supportiveness seems likely to be differentially effective, especially if the support offered is discrepant in any significant way from the survivor's expectations. For example, a woman who has suffered repeated victimizations and feels helpless in the face of her difficulties may feel unsupported and misunderstood by a counselor who says, "Everything will be all right." The importance of seeking the right words remains paramount.

FOLLOW-UP COUNSELING
FOR INDIVIDUALS AND GROUPS

Most rape crisis centers offer and recommend short-term follow-up counseling. Follow-up counseling may be provided to individuals or to groups. If individual, the counselor is usually a professional (e.g., social worker, psychologist, psychiatrist). Groups may be led by either a professional or a trained peer. For both sorts of counseling, the time frame may be set (usually at about 12 weeks for crisis counseling) or open-ended. Investigation is needed into whether one type of crisis counseling is more effective for certain survivors than another. For example, is the follow-up counseling advocated by Burgess and Holmstrom (1974), which focuses on the immediate issues relating to the rape event, more effective for certain individuals than the non-directive approach taken by Symonds (1975, 1976), which includes specific advice to the police and to others dealing with the survivor, but not to the survivor herself? In Symonds' model, referrals for follow-up care are made only when the survivor makes specific requests.

If the client does not want to, or is unable to see a counselor in person, individual telephone counseling is often arranged. This form of treatment is best suited for those survivors who do not have access to health care facilities or who would feel uncomfortable discussing intimate details about the rape or sexual matters with the therapist in person.

Group therapy is another option available for rape survivors. While it does not provide the one-to-one attention given to patients in individual counseling, it does have other advantages. Relative to individual therapy, in the group situation the survivor is likely to feel less isolated and to understand more directly that other people have undergone an experience like her own. The sense of social support provided by groups is one of its most important features, an aspect which seems likely to be of special benefit for women who lack social support in their lives. Women whose experiences are distinct from those of most rape survivors (e.g., incest, gang rape) may not derive the same sense of social support from the group, since they will not find others who shared their experience. Women with severe psychological problems (e.g., psychosis, alcoholism) are also not likely to participate effectively in a group of normal women. Ideally, patients in groups receive peer as well as professional support.

Providing counseling to significant others represents another sort of follow-up care. Such intervention enable significant others (e.g., husband, boyfriend, parents, etc.) to discuss their own feelings about the rape and also provide them with information on what the survivor is experiencing.

Finally, long-term therapy represents another possibility. Short-term counseling of rape survivors has focused on issues relating to the rape and typically has not attempted to delve into further problems. For survivors who experience difficulty in recovery or who exhibit signs of pre-existing psychological disorders, long-term therapy may be indicated.

The treatment alternatives outlined here reflect the notion that "good" care will enable an individual to give voice to her rape experiences within a context designed to promote understanding. The capacity for empathy and a shared sense of what it means to be raped would seem to be the essential ingredients for effective intervention.

CONCLUSION

The act of definition empowers the word chooser and, to the extent meanings are shared, informs the recipient about the speaker's beliefs and by inference, his or her motives. Rape is an interpersonal violation, perpetrated by men against women, girls and occasionally against other males. Issues of definition are especially relevant because, unlike other victimizing events, the act, de-contextualized, stripped of its aggressive intent, may mimic an act of intimacy, of consensual physical closeness. However, to de-contextualize rape in this fashion is to render it entirely meaningless. As any human rape survivor knows, such an event would not be a rape. Because words carry connotative meaning, and because word choices may be motivated by more than the desire to be clear, the choice of words whose meanings are distorted or misapplied must be examined.

Whether we are dealing with a woman who describes a rape as "making love" or with an "objective" scientist who presents information on forced copulation in animals and titles his paper, "Rape as a reproductive strategy: Our evolutionary legacy," we are obliged to acknowledge the function these linguistic choices serve. Joan protected herself from the full emotional impact of what was done to her by calling it "making love." Thiessen (1983), in his paper titling, can be assumed to have less at risk emotionally than Joan, who seeks a name for her experience. Nonetheless, he deliberately invokes the full connotative weight of rape and couches it in a positive context — as a "reproductive strategy, our evolutionary legacy." Strategies and legacies are connotatively positive; thus rape is decontextualized, functionally redefined.

Three years before the publication of *1984*, with its attention to the empowering effects of language, George Orwell wrote, "The slovenliness of our language makes it easier for us to have foolish thoughts" (cited in *Time*, November 28, 1983, p. 47). Perhaps, sociobiologists, victimized by linguistic slovenliness, have been led astray by the urge to sensationalize otherwise less arresting ideas. However, there is a deception worthy of Orwell's "Newspeak" inherent in such word usage. It bespeaks a lack of careful thought about the power of words to structure thoughts and to shape feelings and the importance of the search for words that will inform when one means to inform and inflame only when one means to inflame.

The use of language that distorts meaning is the embodiment of propaganda. Linguistic distortions or propaganda flourish in the context of illusions — here the illusions of positive importance created by placing rape in the context of evolutionary achievements. One can only hope that a commitment to meaningful language can do as well, and that attention to the painful reality of human rape will help to dispel the illusion created by those sociobiologists who have used the word *rape* to describe the behavior of non-human species. This advocacy for attention to semantics is far from trivial; for ultimately, language is our unique evolutionary legacy.

REFERENCES

Abarbanel, G. (1976). Helping victims of rape. *Social work*, 21, 478–482.

Bard, M. (1976). The rape victim: Challenge to the helping systems. *Victimology: An International Journal*, 1(2), 263–271.

Baron, L.C. (1984). Does rape contribute to reproductive success? Evaluation of sociobiological theories of rape. Paper presented at the Eastern Sociological Society meeting, Boston, Mass., Mar. 10, 1984.

Berger, V. (1977). Man's trial, woman's tribulation: Rape cases in the courtroom. *Columbia Law Review*, 77(1), 1–103.

Bleier, R. (1984). *Science and gender: A critique of biology and its theories on women.* New York: Pergamon Press.

Brodyaga, L., Gates, M., Singer, S., Tucker, M. and White, R. (1975). *Rape and its victims: A report for citizens, health facilities, and criminal justice.* Law Enforcement Assistance Administration, U.S. Government Printing Office.

Brownmiller, S. (1975). *Against our will: Men, women and rape.* New York: Bantam Books.

Burgess, A.W. and Holmstrom, L.L. (1974). Crisis and counseling requests of rape victims. *Nursing Research, 23*(3), 196–202.

Corckhuff, R.R. and Pierce, R. (1967). Differential effects of therapists' race and social class upon patient depth of self-exploration in the initial clinical interview. *Journal of Consulting Psychology, 31*, 632–634.

Firestone, S. (1971). On American Feminism. In V. Gornick and B.K. Moran (Eds.), *Woman in sexist society: Studies in power and powerlessness.* New York: New American Library.

Hagen, R. (1979). *The biosexual factor.* New York: Doubleday.

Katz, S. and Mazur, M. (1979). *Understanding the rape victim: A synthesis of research findings.* New York: Wiley and Sons.

MacKinnon, C. (1982). Feminism, Marxism, method and the state: An agenda for theory. *Signs, 7*, 515–544.

Mizio, E. (1972). White worker–minority client. *Social Worker, 17*(3), 82–126.

Peters, J.J., Meyer, L.C., and Carroll, N.E., (1976). *The Philadelphia assault victim study.* Final report from NIMH, RO 1MH21304, 6/30/76.

Schuker, E. (1979). Psychodynamics and treatment of sexual assault victims. *Journal of the American Academy of Psychoanalysis, 7*(4), 533–573.

Shields, S.A. (1975). Functionalism, Darwinism and the Psychology of Women. *American Psychologist, 30*, 739–754.

Shields, W.M. and Shields, L.M. (1983). Forcible rape: An evolutionary perspective. *Ethology and Sociobiology, 4*, 115–136.

Silverman, D. (1977). First do no more harm: Female rape victims and the male counselor. *American Journal of Orthopsychiatry, 47*(1), 91–96.

Symonds, M. (1975). Victims of violence: Psychological effects and after-effects. *American Journal of Psychoanalysis, 35*, 19–26.

Symonds, M. (1976). The rape victim: Psychological patterns of response among victims of rape. *American Journal of Psychoanalysis, 36*(1), 27–34.

Thiessen, D. (1983). Rape as a reproductive strategy: Our evolutionary legacy. Paper presented at the American Psychological Association meeting, Los Angeles, Calif.

Thornhill, R. and Thornhill, N.W. (1983). Human rape: An evolutionary analysis. *Ethology and Sociobiology, 4*, 137–173.

Vontress, C.E. (1971). Racial differences: Impediments to rapport. *Journal of Counseling Psychology, 18*, 7–13.

Williams, C.C. and Williams, R.A. (1973). Rape: A plea for help in the hospital emergency room. *Nursing Forum, 12*(4), 388–401.

Woolf, V. (1935). *A room of one's own.* New York: Harcourt Brace.

EPILOGUE

Ethel Tobach

AMERICAN MUSEUM OF NATURAL HISTORY

and

Suzanne R. Sunday

MANHATTANVILLE COLLEGE

This is a statement which is not a "data" paper. There is a great value placed on scientific presentations which offer data to support the statements made. This is a highly desirable *sine qua non* of the method of communication among scientists. Sometimes, however, there are no "data." This is especially true when the problem being discussed was previously formulated so that the questions being asked could not yield data that would be pertinent to new discussions. A scientific discussion about rape presents such a problem.

For most of the history of the study of rape, questions were formulated in ways that (1) denied the possibility that rape was a behavior pattern derived from societal relationships among women and men; and (2) did not recognize the corollary of that denial, that is, that the victims of rape could not participate in the yielding of reliable and valid data, and that the perpetrators of rape could not be an easily accessible source of data. Until fairly recently, given the position of women in most societies, rape was not seriously considered as a topic of study except within the rubric of crime in general. Some of the most recent attempts to analyze rape are also based on the conclusion that rape is not derived from societal processes. This recent history, written by sociobiologists, instead portrays the primary process as an evolutionary one. In this book, we present the tenets of sociobiology as they relate to rape. In this chapter, we will discuss some additional implications of the sociobiological approach to the etiology of rape and the sociobiological program for treatment and prevention.

Because the premise on which our discussion rests is that rape and the study of rape are societal phenomena particular to the human species, we will also examine the scientific community itself as it studies rape, particularly that segment of the scientific community that presents the sociobiology of rape. To do the latter, we have chosen an interview with Dr. Thiessen (see Prologue, this volume) reported in *The Monitor*, the official newspaper of the American Psychological Association, to demonstrate some of the societal issues raised by the sociobiologists' approach to rape. There is no intention to personalize the discussion by this demonstration. Rather, Dr. Thiessen, as a reputable, well-known researcher in the field of physiological psychology, is representative of widely held views. In a sense, he is the protagonist of the historical drama. As of this writing, he has not indicated to either the reporter who wrote the article, or to the editors of this volume, that anything he said in that interview does not present his opinion correctly.

Any discussion about rape must recognize the confounding and contaminating factors surrounding any raw data. Allan Griswold Johnson points out in his 1980 article on the prevalence of rape in the United States (subsequently his inferences from his data were supported by Russell and Howell, 1983) that:

> Historically, however, the systematic documentation of violence against women has been hard to come by. Statistics on violence against young girls, for example, are either not recorded, or if recorded, not published as in the case of 'statutory rape' in FBI statistics. State legislatures help mask domestic rape by excluding the rape of women by their husbands from criminal statutes. Key figures in the gathering of data on violence — police officers, prosecutors — often behave in ways that discourage women from making their victimication known. (p. 137).

The underreporting of rape is seen especially in the case of "date rape." Recently this phenomenon has become more publicized (for example, a number of papers presented at the 1985 Association for Women in Psychology Conference focused on this topic), but it is still often not labelled as rape by victims, perpetrators, and our legal system. Because the woman had agreed to go out with the man and may have agreed to engage in some sexual activities, it is assumed that the woman consented even if she said "no" at some stage of their activities.

Cann, Calhoun, Selby and King (1981), in their introduction to the *Journal of Social Issues* issue on rape, point out that the difficulties in gathering data result in:

> a system in which the roles of victim and criminal often seem confused. Within the legal system, attention has been focused on the victim's possible role in 'inducing' the rape, while there appears to be much sympathy for the criminal . . . Moreover, rape victims may be stigmatized, forcing them to withdraw and suffer through their victimization with diminished social support.
>
> Some outgrowths of these confusions have been . . . an absence of reliable data on the actual frequency of rape. (p. 2).

(A more detailed discussion of victim-blaming can be found in Danmark and Friedman in this monograph).

Sanday (1981), in her study reported in the same issue of *Journal of Social Issues*, found that the quality of society's structuring of the relation between women and men is clearly correlated not only with the frequency of rape but with the societal treatment of the rapist and the rape victim. (See also the article by the Schwendingers in this monograph and Schwendinger & Schwendinger, 1983).

The failure to take the societal nature of rape into serious consideration is exemplified by the fact that Thornhill and Thornhill (1983) and others base their conclusions concerning human rape on the basis of the FBI Uniform Crime Report (UCR). These statistics reflect *arrests* for various crimes. The UCR, therefore, does not include cases in which the crime is not reported (rape is stated by the FBI as being one of the most underreported crimes) and cases in which no arrest is made. However, Thornhill and Thornhill generalize from the UCR to state, "Poor men seem to be the rapists" (p. 150) and, "Males of racial minorities appear to be overrepresented as rape offenders in the United States, especially blacks" (p. 150–151). While they do mention that wealthier men (who are generally white) are less likely to be caught and tried for crimes than are poor men, they still state that, "when all such factors can be fully eval-

uated, the overrepresentation of low socioeconomic status rape offenders will be highly significant" (p. 152). Given the problems with
the data base, such a conclusion is not warranted and could be
interpreted as class prejudice. For example, Malamuth (1981) cites
Smithyman's 1978 doctoral dissertation as an indication of the bias
in the UCR statistics. Smithyman placed newspaper ads asking
rapists to call him anonymously. Fifty percent of the men who called
him and whom he interviewed, all of whom were "undetected"
rapists, were college educated. This indicates the necessity of cau-
tion in using UCR data. The validity and reliability of UCR data to
support one or another position are not definable at this time and it
may not be productive to analyze them in detail or to make inference from them.

The sociobiologists term rape a "biological phenomenon," that
is, an evolutionary or genetic phenomenon rather than a phenomenon derived from psychological, societal and cultural factors. The
cornerstone of this formulation is their postulate that the human
species is in the class of all polygynous species. Polygynous species
are those in which a male mates with more than one female.
"Humans have morphological, developmental sex ratio, mortality,
senescence, parental general behavioral *correlates* [italics added] of
an evolutionary history of polygyny shown by other polygynous
mammals." (Thornhill & Thornhill, 1983, p. 138). On the basis of
such correlations, sociobiologists conclude that the underlying,
causal processes in social and reproductive behavior are the same
as those of other polygynous mammals; hence, forced copulation
in mammals is the same in the human species. As Harding shows in
her article in this book, much of the data used as "evidence" of rape
in non-human animals are not based on polygynous species but on
monogamous avian species. The relevance of polygyny in mammals or in other animal groups is not clear within the sociobiological formulation. Furthermore, a conclusion based on such
analogous logic is problematic for at least two reasons. First, the
suggestion that human evolutionary history demonstrates
polygyny is purely speculative; there are no data concerning early
hominid mating patterns. Second, correlation does not imply
causality. To arrive at causal explanation, the theory would need to
show how the processes responsible for monogamy, polygyny, or
polyandry are also responsible for, or related to forced copulation
in the animals. As forced copulation has been cited for animals
with varied mating patterns, the analogy is flawed.

The sociobiologists confuse similarity of results with similarity of process. This leads to confusion about the etiology of behavior and thus about the method of "treatment." Two individuals may appear flushed, disoriented, and "high." One, however, is in the process of undergoing a diabetic sugar-imbalance; the other is alcohol-intoxicated. The basic cause of the behavior may be biochemically similar, and the biochemical imbalance caused by diabetes and alcohol may have a similar common final path at the level of neuromuscular, physiological integration which leads to similar vascular, motor, sensory patterns of disorientation and flushing. Nonetheless, the difference in etiology is significant. The similarity in "result" does not in any way determine that the way to "treat" the two disease processes is the same, although a direct biochemical treatment may be similar. The distinction between process and result is clear on a single level, as well as on the level of social behavior. Aggregations of conspecific animals may appear to be the same; a herd of moose may seem similar to an exodus of commuters from a train as they head for the parking lot, but the underlying processes are quite different.

One definition of rape, forced copulation, in an operational style seems to apply to all species; however, the connotations and denotations of human forced copulation are significant discriminanda in defining rape. This becomes clear in a consideration of the etymology of rape which reveals the epistemological, religious and cultural aspects of the history of conception. Above all, an etymological review of the word rape reveals some of the history of the relationships between women and men.

We are aware that in discussing definitions and word usage, we will stimulate the typical response, it is "only" a matter of semantics. The issue of semantics is not trivial; it is a significant, conceptual issue. Language (or semantics) is a reflection of one's thinking about, and understanding of a phenomenon. Particularly in behavioral process analysis, and most particularly in understanding human behavioral process, the semantics of the discussion is inseparable from the formulations of the scientific concepts. Further, in discussion of rape as similar in humans and other animals, the words chosen are particularly informative; that is, their meaning, their denotations and their connotations elicit strong responses (see Prologue, this volume),

The use of the word rape for both people and other animals, by those who see rape as a biological phenomenon, is a reflection of their theoretical base. By anthropomorphizing the behavior of non-human animals, these theories end up zoomorphizing human behavior (see below). We present a different approach to the analysis of forced copulation on both the human and non-human levels. In our approach, rape is solely a human behavior; therefore, we wish to put the issue of the semantics in its proper context: the psychological, societal context. A further discussion of the importance of semantics can be found in Blackman's chapter in this monograph.

The etymology of a word reflects its conceptual history as well as its usage. This is clear in the history of the word rape. The use of the word rape to signify sexual assault and forced copulation may be relatively recent. The *Oxford English Dictionary* (1933) gives 1436 as the date it was so described in the Rolls of Parliament, an early quasi-legal usage. The basic Indo-European form of rape is *rep*, meaning to snatch (Watkins, 1985). In Latin, the verb becomes *rapere*, to seize. Skeat (1968), in his discussion of *rap* (an early form) gives a history in which to seize and carry off is the primary sense, although the additional connotation of haste appears as late as in Chaucer's writings. In general, one is struck by the suggestion of seizing loot, including women, and running off with the spoils in haste. Violence is involved, as is violation; the latter may refer to the violation of ownership or sexual violation, although neither is explicitly stated.

In the history of slavery from its earliest known records to its recent U.S. history, the use of forced copulation by slave owners for personal pleasure (Addams and Wells, 1977) and for increasing the labor supply is a well-documented practice. This was not considered rape. On the other hand, until recently, behavior which was considered to be "sexually suggestive" was labelled as rape if a Black man and a white woman were involved. Such instances frequently resulted in court action or lynching. Today, in the U.S., the probability of a Black man being convicted of raping a white woman is greater than that of a white man raping a Black woman.

Brownmiller (1975) in her book on rape, proposes that the earliest form of rape was practiced early in hominid evolution, with the seizing of a woman by a man to form a reproductive pair. This is obviously conjecture and will remain a problem for investigation. However, throughout slavery and feudalism, women were considered chattel, so that women had no choice concerning their sexual partners. Therefore, no connotative difference was necessary in describing "looting" with or without copulation.

In the middle ages, the custom of abducting women and thus laying the basis for negotiation for property for the consequent enrichment of the abductor, was an accepted way of property aggrandizement (Brownmiller, 1975). Another example of a medieval societal practice which emphasized the irrelevance of the woman's wishes was that of the seigniorage, the prerogative of the feudal lord to copulate with all brides in his fiefdom on their wedding night (for example as in Mozart's "The Marriage of Figaro"). Thus, the concept of rape may have been primarily one of property violation rather than sexual violation.

Brownmiller demonstrates the basis for the concept of rape during the middle ages by describing the "confusion, never quite resolved, as to whether the crime was against a woman's body or a crime against his (the lord's) own estate." (p. 15). The words used for forced sexual activity were apparently the same as those used for sexual intercourse in general, during that period. An early English clear use of rape as a sexual defilement of a woman is cited by Brownmiller with reference to Bracton in the eleventh century. At that time he wrote "an appeal concerning the rape of virgins" which gave the procedure to be followed by a raped woman in her attempt to obtain justice. These instructions were clearly aimed at proving that sexual intercourse had been forced in a bloody and violent manner.

McLaren's book (1983) on the perception of fertility in England from the sixteenth to the nineteenth century, the interdependent relationship of religion, the societal view of gender, science, and the meaning of rape is clear. In the late seventeenth century, popular texts appeared in which it was stated that "the pleasure of women was necessary to ensure conception." (p. 20). Therefore, if a woman conceived after she was raped, this was proof that the copulation had not taken place by force. About that time, medical science was beginning to question the ideas about reproduction which had been based on the writings of Aristotle, Hippocrates, and Galen. The accessibility of new data about embryology and anatomy through the use of the microscope and experimentation made new hypotheses possible. McLaren cites William Harvey as reexamining the old concept of the necessity of having "great enjoyment" (p. 27) during intercourse in order to conceive. Harvey concluded that it was no longer necessary, and so by the nineteenth century the criterion of conception was no longer admissible in the courts as evidence of complicit copulation.

This brief and incomplete review of the etymology of the word rape and its history viewed in the context of the varied patterns of marriage, reproductive bond formation and the relationship of these to property and social organization in the many cultures of today's world, would indicate that the concept and meaning of rape reflects not only the relationship between women and men in regard to gender equality but reflects as well, the cultural concepts of property, power, and politics.

The definitions of rape across human history as well as within the history of any one culture, or in Western industrialized society with its varied subcultures, presents problems for obtaining reliable, valid, and quantifiable data. At this time, these problems have not been solved.

To the sociobiologists, the continuous history of forced copulation as an acceptable way of bringing about reproduction in different cultures attests to the significance of this way of reproduction, and therefore, emphasizes its evolutionary, biological or genetic source. To the sociobiologist, changes in societal acceptance of such behavior simply mean that there may have been strong temporary selection pressures at work to bring about such changes. They would look to famine, disease, war, or some natural catastrophe which affected reproductive success; under such conditions, to perpetuate the species, the constraints on people would be removed. The need and drive to reproduce by any and all means would sanction rape. In times of plenty, health, increasing populations and resources, it would be unnecessary to force copulation and thus the concept of rape would be defined as sexual assault and would be unacceptable to society. The validity of such an analysis is put into question by the sociological and anthropological material presented by the Schwendingers in this volume and others (Benderly, 1982; Sanday, 1981, 1982; also see Shields, Shields, Thornhill, & Thornhill, 1982).

In the sociobiological interpretation of the central role of the reproductive process in the evolution of social behavior (that is, that all individual behavioral patterns are simply the pathway by which the genes are propagated into succeeding generations), (Hamilton, 1964) the issue of rape is viewed in terms of whether or not it is an efficient means of perpetuating the genes of the rapist. If the rapists are successful in doing this, then the "genes" or "culturgens" (Lumsden and Wilson, 1981) for rape will be successfully reproduced in succeeding generations.

The publication of two papers in the same issue of *Ethology and Sociobiology* (1983) on the evolutionary view of rape presented two sociobiological interpretations of rape. Although there are some minor differences in the views held by Thornhill and Thornhill and by Shields and Shields, as they themselves say, the two papers complement each other and present sociobiological interpretations that do not contradict each other. In general, they present a genetic determinist view of rape.

Although some sociobiologists (e.g., Thiessen in his letter to Frieze, see Appendix H) state that genetic determinism does not inherently deny the possibility of modifiability of individual behavior patterns, it is clear from the Shields and Shields and the Thornhill and Thornhill papers that the modification they propose is through modification of the genetic constituency of the human population. They propose to structure societal reaction to rape in such a way that the genes for low threshold for rape are eliminated.

These two presentations in *Ethology and Sociobiology* present rape as a *biological phenomenon.* In understanding the genesis of this phenomenon, they use the concepts of evolutionary and proximate causality. Typically in the literature of evolutionary biology, in ethology, and in sociobiology, "evolutionary" causality is called "ultimate" causality. Mayr's discussion (1982) of ultimate and proximate causality is helpful. "Organisms . . . have two different sets of causes because organisms have a genetic program. Proximate causes have to do with the decoding of the program of a given individual; evolutionary [that is, ultimate] causes have to do with the changes of genetic programs through time, and with the reason for the changes." (p. 68). Mayr credits John Baker (1938) as having made the difference between the two kinds of causality clear, "ultimate causes responsible for the evolution of a given genetic program (selection) and proximate causes responsible, so to speak, for the release of the stored genetic information in response to current environmental stimuli." (p. 162). It is evident from the discussions by Shields and Shields (1983), Thornhill and Thornhill (1983), Mayr, and Baker, that proximate causes, while related in some way to the experience of the individual, are primarily an unfolding of the genetic programs generated in evolutionary history, that is by ultimate causes.

Thornhill and Thornhill term rape a biological phenomenon and therefore a phenomenon derived from both evolutionary and proximate causes. Proximate causality concerns the decoding of the genetic program during the life history of the individual. Rape by an individual is dependent on his life circumstances (that is, social, psychological, cultural) and these are proximate causal factors. At the same time, rape is considered facultative, in that the genetic program expresses itself within the constraints of the situation in which the individual finds himself. Facultative behavior and proximate causality both depend on the genetic programming.

A reader not versed in contemporary evolutionary biological literature might think that if behavior is termed facultative, there are some options open to the individual (see dictionary definition of facultative); that if an individual has options, the constraints of biological (genetic) factors might be attenuated. Actually, the behavior of the rapist is not based on conscious, decision-making, optional behavior according to the sociobiological view. In the analysis offered by the sociobiologists, the individual need not be aware of the ultimate consequences of an act performed; the process is programmed and is independent of individual awareness. Further, the decision-making seen in the individual's performance is either genetically programmed or culturally programmed. However, cultural programming is also genetically determined. ". . . human behavior has evolved by two routes: (1) natural selection acting on behavioral variants *with underlying genetic variants* and (2) cultural selection acting on behavioral variants . . . Both evolutionary routes are expected to result in *behavior that promotes inclusive fitness* (number of descendant and nondescendant kin) of individuals [italics added] . . . Neither cultural nor organic evolution requires that humans be aware of the consequences for reproduction or the behavioral variants upon which these processes act." (Thornhill & Thornhill, 1983, p. 139).

Their formulation of the relation between rape and genetic programming further clarifies their concept of rape:

> ". . . Differences in behavior among human societies or among individuals within a society probably do not reflect underlying genetic differences, but instead reflect only a single general genetic program very indirectly related to behavior differences via the influence of differences in development or general social environment. This means there need not be a fixed genetic programming for a given behavior of humans (e.g. rape) but only a general genetic program whose influence on the phenotype depends on conditions encountered." (p. 140).

In the sociobiological theory proposed by Thornhill and Thornhill and by Shields and Shields, "the general genetic program" which shows variation depending on the circumstances, is the predetermined male reproductive pattern of all sexually reproducing animals. The male must introduce his sperm into as many females as possible; on the other hand, the female's genetic program is to be more selective and cautious about permitting copulation with males. Because of this general genetic programming, men (considered as all males, whether human or not) may adopt different strategies to introduce their sperm into women (that is, all females, including humans).

> . . . *all* men are potential rapists, that is . . . all men possess a conditional mating strategy that includes rape as well as seduction and honest courtship as one of its potential tactics. In addition, the probability of a particular individual raping will be a function of the average genetic cost benefit ratio associated with the particular conditions he faces. (Shields & Shields, 1983 p. 120).

The sociobiologists are well aware that the rapist cannot act without some kind of awareness about the consequence of his act. This type of awareness is related as indicated above, to "facultative" factors, that is, those factors which relate to the individual behavior in the setting in which the rapist finds himself, or because of the complexity of the human species, within the context of the individual's past, present and future (anticipated) experience. Thus, the man may or may not attempt a forced copulation if there are negative facultative conditions, such as fear of punishment, defeat by a stronger woman, revenge by a man who is in some way related to the woman, or distractability, etc. These are the proximate causes which may prevent the forced copulation. Also, the man may not have to resort to forced copulation because of his ability to convince the female to participate in copulation. However, all these "strategies" are a function of the "general genetic program," which though not "fixed" as to the specific behavior is "fixed" by the general "law" of inclusive fitness which programs all behavior.

The conceptualization of facultative factors, proximal and ultimate causality again demonstrates the relationship between language and consciousness in scientific theory.

By dictionary definition, terming rape facultative signifies that it is an option available under the appropriate conditions. But the optionality of the behavior is not really the choice of the individual; the man does not "ultimately" decide what to do on the basis of understanding the options open to him. The "true" options that are available to the rapist are those which have been genetically pro-grammed in evolution and operate without any particular con-sciousness on his part. The development of an individual's behavior pattern which leads to the decision to rape a woman is defined by the genetically determined probability that this will aid the rapist in propagating his genes into the next generation. By terming rape fac-ultative, the sociobiologists do not place the responsibility for rape on the individual and on society because the options that are avail-able are ultimately "evolutionary" or "genetically" determined.

The shift in the meaning of words as they are used by the gen-eral public (e.g. altruism, facultative) is a characteristic of genetic determinists paralleled by their use of anthropomorphic and zoomorphic terms. This type of thinking, based on the emphasis of the "similarities" between people and other animals, is reflected in the anthropomorphic language which attributes human qualities to other animals and is used to describe the apparently similar forced behavior in copulation. The imputing of other animal character-istics to humans is zoomorphism. The two are dialectically related to each other . . . each turns into the other, its opposite.

One possible interpretation of the anthropomorphic language of those studying animal behavior may be the lack of awareness of an underlying philosophical dilemma on the part of the observer. At the same time that one is committed to the view that there is a continuity between humans and all other animals (indeed, plant species), there is a discontinuity which needs to be accommodated. Those who follow some religious philosophies see the philosophy underlying scientific work independent, in the short run, of one's spiritual belief system. In the long run, they see scientific work as an expression of spiritual guidance in the "ultimate" sense, in that people, having souls, are closer to that ultimate spiritual guide. At the same time, they see people as related to other animals, in that people also reveal their baseness, that is animal-like undesirable behavior. Other religious belief systems hold that animals and humans are all part of the same life force and therefore are equivalent. The dominant religious view in Europe and the United States is that sinfulness, baseness, non-human morality are "animal-like," but, we all have something of the animal in us. In both types of belief systems, em-phasizing the continuity of all animals (including the human species), both zoomorphic and anthropomorphic language results.

Contemporary sophisticated thinking can deal with the fact that although we are related in many ways to all living systems, the differences among species are significant. Thus, forced copulation on the part of an animal other than a human will have different underlying processes than that in the human. A female bird which walks and stops and continues walking again as the male bird closes the distance between her and him, and then finally stops, is not being "coy." The underlying processes of the relation between qualities of immediate stimulation and past experience, the hormonal state of the organisms involved, etc. are determined through the total experience of each of those individuals. A Victorian woman, who has been schooled in the work of capturing a man for marriage in order to solve her economic future, uses props and behavior patterns which are very different from those of birds. She may be "coy." In the case of the birds, the "future" of each of the animals' individual survival (obtaining food, protection from predators) is not being planned by increasing the probability of copulation. If the female does not copulate with the male, she will go on to feed herself, and run from predators, etc., as will the male. The Victorian woman would also have survived, but very likely in a marginal way.

The sociobiological argument is that in the case of the people and in the case of the birds their behavior will, if appropriately attuned to the perceptual and social history of the individuals concerned, lead to the increased probability of their having viable offspring which will perpetuate their genes. In both cases, however, the sociobiologists confuse the results of the behavior with the cause of the behavior (see discussion above of ultimate versus proximate causality). In both cases, if the bird responds appropriately and if the woman is in the appropriate societal setting and has had the appropriate socialization, each individual may be "reproductively or genetically fit." Beyond the level of zygote formation, there are significant discontinuities at all succeeding levels of reproduction (Tobach, 1977).

The emphasis on apparent similarities between humans and other species expressed in the language used is also evident in correlational thinking about polygyns. One has only to consider the various forms of parenting and the changes they are undergoing in our contemporary society, as well as the multivariate causal processes underlying senescence and its definition in different societies, to wonder about the meaning of this analogy between human and other polygyns in the animal world. The result of this type of thinking is strongly illustrated by Thornhill and Thornhill's discussion (1983) about the forced copulation of a boss and a secretary or a slave owner and a slave:

Furthermore, copulation by a man with women who depend on him or are under his control (e.g. a male employer copulating with his female secretary or a male slaveowner with his female slave) is not *necessarily* rape (or any other form of sexual conflict) by our definition because the female need not be denied the option of gaining benefits that exceed costs to reproduction (job security or salary (secretary); resources or higher status for self or offspring (slave)). We are not saying that men in powerful positions never rape women dependent upon them. But we limit actual rape in such circumstances to situations in which a copulation is forced in the sense that the female loses her ability to use copulation in her own reproductive interest. This is, the woman herself views the copulation as maladaptive. High status men, however, probably rarely actually rape.

Human males compete with each other for relative status, including wealth and prestige . . . Relative advantage brings with it the resources necessary to rear offspring successfully and thereby brings access to desirable females. (p. 141).

And therefore, these successful men are the men who do not need to rape. Thornhill and Thornhill propose that this competition with its yielding of the prize ("desirable females") to the "best man" has an evolutionary root.

It is a possibility that human rape is simply an inevitable outcome of an evolutionary history in which males were selected to persist in their attempts to copulate and females were selected to discriminate among males and often refuse copulation . . . At the point in human history when retribution from society . . . became a component of the cost/benefit in male decision making about rape as an alternative, those who persisted . . . to the point of rape when costs exceeded benefits would have been outreproduced by males *who adopted rape adaptively* [italics added]. Thus we envision selection acting on human males in evolutionary history in the context of their persistence and forcefulness in copulation attempts." (p. 142).

What are the implications of this genetic determinist view of rape? Both articles in *Ethology and Sociobiology* attempt to present their theory in such a way as to accommodate criticisms of genetic determinism as precluding unmodifiable individual behavior. Thornhill and Thornhill do not propose any program for inhibiting or preventing rape based on their sociobiological analysis of rape. On the other hand, Shields and Shields propose that extreme punishment is the appropriate way to inhibit and prevent rape. The reader should not conclude from this that the Shields and Shields proposal is based on some experiential effect of punishment on individual behavior during the lifetime of the individual. They propose to bring about a decline in rape through genetic intervention. Extreme punishment will be used to delete the alleles (genetic systems) related to rape behavior, and genes for altruistic behavior (based on kinship) would be encouraged.

> ". . . we are postulating a complex genetic substrate contributing to the control of rape in a variety of *unknown* (our emphasis, ET & SS) ways. First, we assume . . . a closed behavioral program linking hostility and female vulnerability with forced copulation. We perceive this connection 'hard-wired' and the genetic substrate encoding it as essentially *fixed* in the human population . . . we view rape as a human universal and on this level, probably recalcitrant to reprogramming via individual experience." (p. 123).

The exact nature of the "extreme punishment" is never made explicit.

The program developed by Shields and Shields for solving the genetically determined problem of rape is to increase the innate threshold for rape by such severe punishment that it would eliminate the individuals with lower thresholds (presumably before they passed on their genes) thus increasing the relative frequency of alleles associated with higher threshold, and thus eventually lowering the occurrence of rape.

> "Extreme punishment . . . would result *not in conscious* (our emphasis, ET & SS) consideration of the genetic effects of the punishment the rapist might expect, but from his evolutionary favored ability to assess female vulnerability *as if* he were aware of such fitness considerations. Thus, if the punishment were sufficiently probable, severe, or both, the costs of rape would almost invariably exceed its benefits and potential rapists would be expected to refrain." (p. 132).

Shields and Shields also propose that by decreasing the probability of rape, not only would the threshold for rape be raised, but by punishment severe enough to eliminate the alleles for lower threshold, the factors that contribute to "male hostility" would be adjusted societally, although they "may be recalcitrant." But the attempt should be made, they say.

At the same time, women should learn to minimize their vulnerability. Lest the reader believe that here at last there is some area of agreement between the sociobiologist and those who view rape as a societal phenomenon, Shields and Shields reveal why they believe these adjustments may be possible. In the sociobiological view, individuals who are closely related are more likely to be altruistic, cooperative, and "kind" to each other. Therefore, the concluding proposal for eliminating rape is based on the notion that closely related people are less likely to rape or be raped. They continue by saying that, "when a society regards the rape of *any* woman the way individuals perceive the rape of their daughters, sisters or mates, and then resists, pursues and punishes the rapists accordingly, rape will cease to be a major problem." (p. 133). The prevalence of incest and wife-raping do not support such a proposal.

The superficial appearance of this program conjures up scenarios of advertisements saying, "This might be your sister" and showing a picture of a badly traumatized woman, followed by another panel advertising for volunteers to pursue and punish the rapists. The appeal to kinship rather than to some more general morality and sense of justice reveals once again the genetic determinist assumptions underlying the program to eliminate rape from the human experience.

The sociobiological view of rape derived from a genetic determinist view of behavior (phylogenetically and ontogenetically) is defended as not ruling out modification of behavior by Thiessen in his letter to Frieze (Appendix H). In that letter, Dr. Thiessen says that his partial aim is to understand rape so that it can be controlled. Another part of his aim appears to be the separation of the sociological and psychological sources from the biological sources. This dichotomization of physiological or biochemical (endocrine, genetic) processes from psychological processes is characteristic of genetic determinists who see the two traditional opposites of nurture/nature, environment/heredity, acquired/innate as two *interacting* entities. The two opposites stand in some quantitative, analyzable arithmetic relationship to each other, leading to the kind of research which seeks to determine *how much* is genetic and *how much* is environmental. In this view, the probability that some significant portion of a behavioral pattern is genetic usually typifies the genetic portion as a limiting, fundamentally (ultimately) determining portion (Tobach, 1972). Many interactionists cite the universality of certain behavior patterns in all human societies as evidence of a "genetic" component (e.g., Eibl-Eibesfeldt, 1970). Does universality attest to the preeminence of the genetic process in "determining" the behavior of human beings?

This attempt to pin behavior into a genetically-determined framework because of universality oversimplifies the "facts" of the quality of being human. Regardless of the culture, for the human being, the species biochemical characteristics, and the sources of energy appropriate to those biochemical characteristics bring about the consequent physiological and behavioral developmental processes which make for the "universality" of human traits. These biochemical characteristics are derived from the genetic and trophic processes which participate in the integration of individuals and their ecological and societal settings. These species characteristics include all the historical, cultural, ontogenetic processes which became integrated in the unique individual organism — the person. At no point is it possible to disengage the interconnected biochemical and experiential processes which produce the individual. Individuals who are not born in the appropriate human environment do not exhibit the universal human characteristics in the same way. Because of the variation in individual histories in varied circumstances, differences and similarities arise.

From the moment the gamete (gene carrying structure) is formed, the changes that take place may or may not be appropriate for the development of species-typical structure or function. In any event, those processes (change) will result in an organism, which in its development, is not the same as any other organism. This variation is an important consideration in the evolutionary process of change. It is also an important expression of the integration of the various levels of organization in the individual and in its relationship to the environment.

The concept of integrative levels does not require a dichotomization of inner processes (e.g., biochemical and physiological) and the outer processes (e.g., the various forms of energy which variably enter the boundaries of the individual at various levels of organization). Quantitative changes on one level result in qualitative changes, interpenetrating subsumed and succeeding levels to varying degrees, depending on how closely or distinctly the levels are structured. The levels approach formulates the problem of the relationship of genes to any other level of organization differently than the interactionist approach. In the integrative levels approach, the biochemical/genetic level is integrated in other organismic levels in the manner described above. These integrated relationships can only be understood developmentally (as a process), by observing changes under varying conditions, at as many levels of organization as possible.

This approach should be very familiar to the geneticists who work with "gene expression," particularly in botany. The problem facing the behavioral scientist is that to carry out such research in complex organisms, such as mammals (and certainly in the most complex species of all, humans), is a difficult and time/money/effort expensive program of research. This would daunt any scientist. However, it is possible to attack pieces of this program, as for example, by research with animals well-suited to research in the controlling conditions of scientific investigation.

It is also possible to use "experiments in nature" to elucidate the principles which may operate to bring about certain types of changes, e.g., the so-called biochemical inborn errors in which supplementation of the food (biochemical) intake leads to the correction of enzyme or other protein error to bring about startling changes in the behavior or morphology of the individual. Frequently, such corrections are the domain of medical science, where the aim is to "cure" the patient. The use of the data to be gathered from that patient at every level of organization (biochemical, endocrinological, physiological, behavioral, and societal) are rarely done, and then usually in unsystematic fashion. The problem of carrying out such research systematically would raise serious and important ethical issues. For example, we could declare any child with Down's Syndrome a national treasure to be studied on every level so as to understand how that chromosomal difference brings about a difference in morphology and behavior. However, the informed consent issue is the simplest one confronting a society in which the financial resources for such work are severely restricted in the face of other demands on the national income. Alternatively, geneticists have attempted to produce mice with a trisomy equivalent to Down's in an attempt to explicate the interpretation of the biochemical level in the physiological and behavioral levels (For want of a mightier mouse, 1984).

The integrative levels approach, by proposing that each level of organization requires its own principles of investigation, as well as its own techniques and instrumentation, obviates the confusion and difficulties of integrating biochemical, physiological, and behavioral levels. Rape is a phenomenon on the behavioral, societal level of organization, and as such, integrates all subsumed levels (biochemical, physiological). In other words, it is understood that for the rapist to be able to violently assault a woman sexually, biochemical and physiological processes must be involved. To understand the etiology of rape, one needs to know the relevant significance of lower levels such as the biochemical level which includes hormonal, neurotransmitter, etc. processes. One must analyze the integration of such levels to understand how the behavioral and societal levels emerge. This requires an intensive, longitudinal investigation. The individual's life history, therefore, becomes paramount in attempting to understand rape. Only then would it be possible to develop a program of inhibition and eventual elimination of the behavior. The levels approach could not rely on "unknown" genetic processes (see Shields and Shields) to develop a research program to control rape.

For example, the sociobiologic view leads Thiessen to state that most rapes resemble the demographics of mutually agreed upon sexual intercourse. (See above for apparent similarities between behavior patterns and assumptions about their underlying causal processes). In this view, the article by Lucinda Franks in the *New York Times* would seem to support the sociobiological view of rape as an event which should be evaluated in terms of the likelihood of preventing the woman from reproducing in the future. The article appeared shortly after a woman had died while resisting a rape. Before she died, the rape victim said that she would have submitted to rape rather than risk being killed. That most victims may feel that way is evident by the data cited by Detective Ellen King, a sex crimes expert in the New York City Policy Department. She said that most sex crimes do not end in the death of the victim.

The victim of sexual assault, threat, or actual forced copulation is in a situation which is life-threatening, job-threating, societal approbation-threatening (when in a societal setting in which it is accepted that a woman who is raped "brought it on herself"). In other words, individual survival is the proximate and ultimate motivation. This needs to be taken into account when analyzing such data. That individual survival is only motivated by species survival is unprovable. Such a view rests on the assumption that the individual human being is carrying out a genetically programmed decision in which consciousness and awareness may play no part.

A further reading of the reports of victims and almost-victims of violent sexual assault reveals the level of integration on which they are operating. The behavior of the intended victim is a function of the ontogenetic history of the woman's socialization. Her response may be one of submission. The sociobiologist would say that this woman does not carry the genes which are to be encouraged, that is, she is a vulnerable individual. Shields and Shields would have society eliminate those alleles. They do not say how this would be done. On the other hand, viewing the woman's behavior as derivative, psychosocial processes, the socialization necessary to change her becomes accessible to the intended victim, and the possibility of rape is averted. The sociobiologist would say that the woman who responds appropriately, thwarts the rapist, and lives to reproduce, will add her genes to the population pool and thus reduce the reproductive fitness of intending rapists in future generations.

The probability that most women can indeed be socialized to prepare themselves as best as possible to prevent rape may be projected as fairly high, as in any population, there is a distribution of individuals who are more or less able to become socialized in that fashion. In this way, the probability that rape would be eliminated or prevented would rely on the ability of the human population to be truly human: to be able to develop mores and behavioral patterns which structure society in such a way as to prevent rape. Just as the concept of rape underwent changes in the past, it can be further modified, without resorting to "unknown" genetic processes and without waiting for future generations to be changed.

The solution to the Darwinian paradox offered by the sociobiologists has stimulated criticism from those who argue against the reductionism of sociobiology (Lewontin, Rose and Kamin, 1984), those who support the integrative levels approach (Tobach, 1982; Tobach and Greenberg, 1984), and those who find the effect of sociobiological theory on other disciplines and on society seriously counterproductive (Rose, 1982). The application of sociobiological theory to rape stimulates criticism by those who see genetic determinism as justification for pejorative formulations about women, minorities, nuclear war and other contemporary societal issues. The phenomenon of the arousal of intense discussion and criticism in a significant sector of the scientific community suggests that there are corollary issues in the sociology of science to be examined.

These issues are best exemplified by a discussion of the interview that Dr. Thiessen gave to *The Monitor* (see beginning of this chapter), the letter which Thiessen wrote to Frieze (Appendix H), and other statements that are in the Appendix. In all these documents, the following issues emerge:

1) The issue of freedom of inquiry
2) The politicization of science
3) Sensitivity to sexism in the conduct of science and professional affairs.

Several of the critics of Dr. Thiessen's presentation made it clear that they were not attempting to censor him. There is no question about the right of Dr. Thiessen to have access to journals, podia, media, research resources, etc. In all these cases, the material he presents is judged on its merit, validity and reliability. There is no question about his right, as well as others, to espouse hereditarian, interactionist, or any other theory of behavior. However, with the case of a presentation at the American Psychological Association, there are societal constraints which need to be considered.

A scientific meeting is designed to facilitate communication among scientists about the "state of the art," about the current issues confronting and interesting the scientific community; and to stimulate thinking and planning of future investigations and development of theory. This gives the governing bodies (conference organizing bodies) of the organization a serious responsibility to be discharged. It also calls upon the scientist who is presenting material, and those who arrange for the material to be presented at those meetings, to consider their responsibilities to their colleagues very carefully. At a scientific meeting, 1) the presentation of controversial material should be labelled as such to begin with; 2) the presentation should clearly set forth its particular viewpoints; and 3) participants at the Convention should be given the opportunity to hear other positions involved, or be made knowledgeable about where such material is obtainable. This does not mean that one always must have "both sides" presented at the same session. It means that all precautions should be taken that the psychologists who attend the APA not be misinformed, or incompletely informed, about the significance of the presentation in ethical, scientific and societal terms.

Thus, if Dr. Thiessen submits a title of a talk on a sensitive issue, rape, the governance group responsible for the program should have been informed by Dr. Thiessen as to the controversial nature of his approach. If Dr. Thiessen was not aware of it, then the governance bodies should have been sensitive to the possible significance of the presentation.

We are suggesting that the responsibility for that presentation rests on the shoulders of all those who had anything to do with the final publication of the title of the talk and its presentation. This view is derived from the nature of the phenomenon of rape and of its study; it is a human societal problem.

How is it that psychology, in its "mainstream" approach to behavior, as exemplified in its introductory textbooks, in its materials as a professional and scientific organization, and in the persons of those most responsible for presenting the "face" of psychology is unaware of the controversy surrounding sociobiology? How is it that all those who knew of the title and subject matter of Dr. Thiessen's talk were so insensitive to the issue — that the concept of rape is not like the concept of rehabilitation after stroke or psychomotor adjustment in dial turning? Years ago, a paper on the biological basis of intelligence or the evolutionary legacy of eugenics would not have stimulated the noticeable response that it would today. The psychological community had to have participated in the debates of heredity/environment in intelligence determination and been witness to the development of the civil rights movement to become sensitive to racism. It would appear that those events did not result in any real change in the views of the majority of psychologists. On the licensing examinations, on the doctoral examinations, in the textbooks, the interaction idea (that is, the quantification of a genetic component and an environmental component of intelligence) is still the dominant one. As explained above, this view places the burden on the psychologist to determine how much is hereditarily determined and how much is environmentally determined. This view, which portrays the gene as the limiting factor in modifiability, is still the justification for societal policies and interpretations of individual differences which discriminate against minorities.

It is our view that given this preeminent view in psychology, it is understandable that the title of Dr. Thiessen's talk and his abstract went unnoticed by most of the people who saw them. The written and spoken statements of those who protested and defended Dr. Thiessen support our view. An analysis of the interview with Dr. Thiessen; his statements in his letters; the statements in Dr. Miller's letter; even the protests (which place the justifiable and appropriate emphasis on the inflammatory title and the anti-woman connotation of his remarks and his title) show that none of these place the responsibility for the incident on the total psychological community. The community appears to have abdicated its responsibility for examining the theoretical foundations of psychological science in the light of its implications for society.

This problem within the psychological community is explicated in the formulation of the response at the APA as reported by Susan Cunningham. Ms. Cunningham's reportage is faultless; it is because she reflects so well the dominant viewpoint of the psychological community that her article is noteworthy. We would not doubt in any way that most of the attendants at the Convention viewed the reaction of Division 35 of the APA and of the Association of Women in Psychology as well as of other women and men, as "a minor controversy," and almost as though one would have to be a feminist to be antagonized by the title and substance of Dr. Thiessen's talk. We believe Ms. Cunningham was right; more's the pity.

In the article, the issue of freedom of inquiry was raised. Freedom of inquiry carries with it responsibility to the society which makes that inquiry possible. Science is a societal enterprise; as such, it is impossible to separate it from other societal processes. That is, it is impossible to consider that science is independent of "politics."

It is understandable, however, that Dr. Thiessen is concerned about the effects that political movements have on science; it is probably for this reason that he is concerned about the "depoliticization" of rape. Unfortunately, Dr. Thiessen does not give us his opinions of the effects that politics have had on science. The analysis of gender discrimination in the training, employment, research support and recognition of women in science is well-told and need not be elaborated here (see *Psychology of Women Quarterly*). But this politicization of gender discrimination in the institutions of science also appears in the very formulation of research questions and theories underlying the research. Dr. Thiessen's plea to depoliticize the study of rape may be seen as a plea to "desocialize" rape — which, in the opinion of the editors of this volume, is not possible to do.

The dictionary definition (Webster's, 1965) of "politicization" and "politics" may give us a clue to Dr. Thiessen's view of the fundamental character of rape. To politicize is to "give a political tone or character to: to bring within the realm of politics." "Politics" is defined as (first meaning), "the art or science of government: a science dealing with the regulation and control of men [sic] in society . . . the art of adjusting and ordering relationships between individuals and groups in a political community."

It would appear that to depoliticize the subject of rape is to remove it from the societal, political arena. In which realm should it be? In his letter to Dr. Frieze (Appendix H), Dr. Thiessen indicates that part of his aim is to prevent rape from taking place through sociological, economic and psychological conditions. One would assume this would require some change of those conditions or intervention. It is difficult to see how this could be done apolitically.

It is possible that Dr. Thiessen was concerned about another aspect of politicization of the study of rape. Perhaps the problem is that women, as critics, might give a political tone to the study of rape. If that is the problem, Dr. Thiessen may be concerned about the fact that as women have been the most frequent victims of rape behavior, there is a possibility that their approach will be contaminated by the human error. This may be his fear. It is clear that this fear exists in the reaction of women to how men approach the study of rape. As men are virtually the sole perpetrators who presumably do not want to be punished, the analysis and the study of rape by men as a beneficent activity for the human species is equally likely to be contaminated. In this apparent standoff, the search for understanding must lead to a viewing of the problem with a minimum of bias. This can best be accomplished by clear, non-sensationalized statements by all concerned with the societal implication of the theory underlying the research.

On another level of interpretation, Dr. Thiessen's plea may be seen to be related to the idea that "objectivity" in science is obtainable if the scientific work is made in some way independent of the societal nature of the scientific activities and theory. "Objectivity" is at all times a relative quality depending on the stage of knowledge about a subject at any particular time, upon the feasibility of minimizing the human error in the investigation being undertaken, and upon the awareness of those involved in the scientific pursuit about possible contaminations that may affect efforts at "objectivity." In the case of human behavior, the human being looking at other human beings must always work with that contaminating factor. Therefore, it is always necessary to be aware of these possibilities and attempt to control the factors as much as possible.

It is at all times difficult to keep on the alert to the constraints of these considerations. An example is the problem presented by the data about rape available for analysis and interpretation. As indicated above, our position is that there are very little reliable and valid data about the occurrence of rape, or any of the significant demographic characteristics, etiological processes and other related factors. This is recognized by all as fact; even Thornhill and Thornhill indicate their awareness of the problem. "The studies we examined in our attempt to test predictions do not classify data in ways conducive to rigorous testing . . . Furthermore, the data in the rape literature that we used in testing predictions contain many biases that will need to be eliminated in future work." (p. 168). Despite these difficulties, Thornhill and Thornhill have no compunction about "testing" their predictions derived from their theoretical approach by using these "biased" data.

Another indication of the difficulty of remaining alert to all the subtleties of our own personal errors of observation is the statement made by Dr. Thiessen at the end of his interview with Susan Cunningham. Dr. Thiessen suggests that the behavior of the rapist also may improve the woman's reproductive fitness. He says, "there may also be sexual and reproductive facets (of rape) geared toward the reproductive facility of women." The dictionary definition (Webster's, 1965) of facility is as follows, "1. The quality of being easily performed; freedom from difficulty, ease. 2. Ease in performance; readiness proceeding from skill or use. Dexterity (practice gives a wonderful facility). 3. Easiness to be persuaded: readiness, compliance, pliancy."

This view of the end result of rape (that is, the improvement of the women's reproductive fitness) is significant when combined with his saying, "I'm not saying it's not an aggressive or violent act, but I'm saying there's been an overemphasis on this." Purposefully, or inadvertently, he places the reader in the position of trading off the violence which should not be emphasized for the reproductive fitness which comes about through the rape experience.

There is little evidence or discussion about the possible relationship between an individual's philosophical approach to scientific issues and to societal issues. Generally speaking, it is assumed that the "rebel" in science is at least an eccentric in society. However, it is also possible that the rebel in science is a conforming conservative in the societal setting. In Dr. Thiessen's written statement, and in the interview, he makes it clear that he subscribes to the theoretical formulations of the sociobiologists, probably those of Thornhill and Thornhill and of Shields and Shields. Dr. Thiessen makes a strong statement to the effect that he believes that being a determinist does not preclude the possibility of non-genetic modifiability of behavior. Unfortunately, we have only the Shields and Shields proposal of extreme punishment to modify the behavior on the basis of evolutionary theory. That has been the hallmark of "treating" or "solving" the problem in the past. This has not been successful in preventing or inhibiting rape in the past and the "fact" that the pattern has an evolutionary (genetically determined) aspect does not strengthen credibility in the proposed solution.

In the interview, Dr. Thiessen also notes that it appears to him that in many respects the pattern of rape behavior resembles the typical societal activity around sexual behavior. It may be that in U.S.A. society, in the typical consenting sexual relationship, the pattern is one of men being older than women. In the rape situation, it is also possible to view these facts in the context that in this society, the right of men to obtain sex either by force or by consent is equally acceptable to society. That these two "facts" make rape an evolutionarily adaptive behavior pattern is questionable. For example, the question of the incest taboo is frequently discussed among sociobiologists as an example of the genetic imperative to protect the gene pool by increasing variation; as variation is decreased in incestuous reproduction, it is forbidden. However, in recent years, the increase of reported sexual abuse and forced sexual intercourse in incestuous relations in the United States (e.g. Thorman, 1983) is being discussed with alarm. If indeed, incestuous relationships are frequent, perhaps as frequent as "normal" reproduction, does this then signify that incest is evolutionarily adaptive? The universality of human behavior patterns is as much a reflection of the universality of the human societal commonalities as it is the universality of the genetic configuration.

The issue that is political in this discussion is: what is the aim of the question, is it inherited or is it acquired? This question is one which primarily arises from societal processes. There is a component of curiosity; the human characteristic is to ask, "why." This is the characteristic which is not always encouraged. Why does one seek to answer the question of the relative amounts of genetic and other influences in a human behavior pattern? This has been discussed at length by many; in general, there are good reasons to be alerted to the need to understand how the question relates to the societal organization in which the question is asked (Lewontin, Rose and Kamin, 1984). What are the motivations of the people asking such questions? What are the resulting societal policy decisions based on them? Where and how do they relate to the morality, ethics and value systems of the people involved? These are questions which need to be answered in each instance. This requires serious and well-formulated investigations which are in the domain of many disciplines and would require an interdisciplinary study by those in the humanities and in the social sciences. Therefore, barring such an intensive investigation, one cannot attribute any particular motive to Dr. Thiessen, or to any of the others who subscribe to genetic determinist views of behavior, particularly human behavior.

In this attempt to place the responsibility equally on the shoulders of all psychologists for the need to be alert to the societal implications of our work, we wish to indicate that there is a possible relationship between the societal context in which science is done and the type of science which is done. This awareness may go a long way to raise our consciousness about our responsibilities. As scientists we are fortunate; we do the work we love to do. Most of the population, in order to survive, does work that is at the least uninteresting, and at the worst, stressful and unpleasant. The entire society supports science. Science needs to support all of society.

REFERENCES

Addams, J. and Wells, I. B. (1977). *Lynching and rape: An exchange of views.* New York: AIMS.

Benderly, B. L. (1982). Rape-free or rape-prone. *Science '82, 3,* 40–43.

Brownmiller, S. (1975). *Against our will: Men, women and rape.* New York: Bantam Books.

Cann, A., Calhoun, L. G., Selby, J. W. and King, H. E. (1981). Rape: A contemporary overview and analysis. *Journal of Social Issues, 37,* 1–4.

Cunningham, S. (1983, October). Rape speech angers women. *The Monitor,* p. 22.

Eibl-Eibesfeldt, I. (1970). *Ethology: The biology of behavior.* New York: Holt, Rinehart and Winston.

For want of a mightier mouse. (1984, October 13). *Science News, 126,* 237.

Franks, L. (1984, December 27). When facing the rapist: Is resistance a strategy? *New York Times,* pp. C1, C3.

Hamilton, W. D. (1964). The genetic theory of social behavior, I, II. *Journal of Theoretical Biology, 7,* 1–52.

Johnson, A. G. (1980). On the prevalence of rape in the United States. *Signs, 6,* 136–146.

Lewontin, R. C., Rose, S., and Kamin, L. J. (1984). *Not in our genes: Biology, ideology and human nature.* New York: Pantheon Books.

Lumsden, C. J. and Wilson, E. O. (1981). *Genes, mind, and culture.* Cambridge, MA: Harvard University Press.

Malamuth, N. M. (1981). Rape proclivity among males. *Journal of Social Issues, 37,* 138–157.

Mayr, E. (1982). *The growth of biological thought.* Cambridge, MA: Belknap Press of Harvard University Press.

McLaren, A. (1983). *Reproductive rituals: The perception of fertility in England from the sixteenth century to the nineteenth century.* New York: Methuen.

Oxford English dictionary (1933). Oxford: Oxford University Press.

Rose, S. (Ed.). (1982). *Against biological determinism.* London: Allison & Busby.

Russell, D. E. H. and Howell, N. (1983). The prevalence of rape in the United States revisited. *Signs, 8,* 688–695.

Sanday, P. R. (1981). The socio-cultural context of rape: A cross-cultural study. *Journal of Social Issues, 37,* 5–27.

Sanday, P.R. (1982). Reply. *Science 82, 3,* 16.

Schwendinger, Julia and Schwendinger, Herman. (1983). *Rape and inequality.* Beverly Hills, CA: Sage Publishers.

Shields, W. M. & Shields, L. M. (1983). Forcible rape: An evolutionary perspective. *Ethology and Sociobiology, 4,* 115–136.

Shields, W. M., Shields, L. M., Thornhill, R. and Thornhill, N. W. (1982). What causes rape? A dissenting view. *Science 82, 3,* 16.

Skeat, W. W. (1910). *An etymological dictionary of the English language.* Rev. & enl. ed. Oxford: Oxford University Press.

Thorman, G. (1983). *Incestuous families.* Springfield, MA: Charles C. Thomas.

Thornhill, R. & Thornhill, N. W. (1983). Human rape: An evolutionary analysis. *Ethology and Sociobiology, 4,* 137–173.

Tobach, E. (1972). The meaning of cryptanthroparion. In L. Ehrman, G. Omenn, and E. Caspari (Eds.), *Genetics, environment and behavior* (pp. 219–239). New York: Academic Press.

Tobach, E. (1977). Femaleness, maleness and behavior disorders in nonhumans. In E. S. Gomberg and V. Franks (Eds.), *Gender and disordered behavior* (pp. 37–68). New York: Brunner/Mazel.

Tobach, E. (1982). The synthetic theory of evolution. In G. Tembrock and H. D. Schmidt (Eds.), *Evolution and determination of animals and human behavior* (pp. 27–39). Berlin: Vep Deutscher Verlag der Wissenschaften.

Tobach, E. and Greenberg, G. (1984). T. C. Schneirla's contributions to the concept of levels of integration. In G. Greenberg and E. Tobach (Eds.), *Behavioral evolution and integrative levels.* Hillsdale, NJ: Lawrence Erlbaum.

Watkins, C. (Ed.). (1985). *The American heritage dictionary of Indo-European roots.* Boston: Houghton Mifflin Co.

Webster's new international . . . dictionary (1965). 3rd ed. unabridged. (1965). Springfield, MA: G.C. Merriam Co.

APPENDICES

APPENDIX A

Barnard College
Columbia University
606 West 120th Street
New York, New York 10027
Department of Psychology

July 26, 1983

Dr. David Miller
Department of Psychology
University of Connecticut
Box U–20
Storrs, Connecticut 06268

Dear Dr. Miller:

I would like to bring to your attention, in your role as program chair, the title of a paper that is offensive to women (and, I hope, to many men as well).

Delbert Thiessen is delivering a Fellows' address called "Rape as a reproductive strategy: Our evolutionary legacy." This title presents sexual violence against women as somehow acceptable or justifiable since rape is merely a reproductive strategy that is part of our evolutionary heritage. The title is sensationalistic, provocative, and designed to attract as wide an audience as possible from the press, and presumably male colleagues. Although Thiessen may be unaware of it, he exploits women in order to draw attention to his talk — a repugnant instance of sexist advertising.

I would also like to point out that at least some well-known workers in the same field are much more careful than Thiessen in their scientific communications. I am referring to the work of McKinney and his colleagues, who explicitly repudiate the use of the term rape, and they also refer to the apparently forced copulations they observe as species-specific. (See, for example, Cheng, K.M., Burns, J.T., & McKinney, F. Forced copulation in captive mallards: II. Temporal factors. *Animal Behaviour,* 1982, *30,* 695–699.)

When saying that a scientist should not say something, I am indeed concerned about the academic freedom of the scientist. Although I have serious doubts about the intellectual position that Thiessen appears to be taking, I uphold his right to express his ideas. However, he has no right to be offensive to a particular group in society in expressing those ideas.

Sincerely,

Lila Ghent Braine
Professor and Chair

LGB: nw
cc: Allan Mirsky
    Delbert Thiessen

APPENDIX B

The University of Connecticut
Storrs, Connecticut 06268

The College of
   Liberal Arts and Sciences
Department of Psychology

August 2, 1983

Dr. Lila Ghent Braine
Barnard College
Department of Psychology
Columbia University
606 West 120th Street
New York, NY 10027

Dear Dr. Braine:

Thank you for your letter of July 26 in which you expressed objection and concern regarding the title of Del Thiessen's invited fellows address, "Rape as a Reproductive Strategy: Our Evolutionary Legacy." I understand why you (and probably others) are offended by this title and its possible implications, which you spelled out in your letter.

I agree that the title is provocative (though I doubt that the intent was to draw *media* coverage). Most speakers want colleagues to attend their talks (especially in Division 6, where attendance tends to be a problem). It is not surprising to use a provocative title to help increase attendance, as is often the case at meetings of other societies that run numerous concurrent sessions, such as the Animal Behavior Society. As to whether or not, Dr. Thiessen's talk is truly sexist (which I hope it will not be), neither you nor I will know until the actual presentation, and then the responsibility will be solely his for defending his views. At this point, I choose neither to endorse nor condemn his chosen title, but, rather, hold in abeyance any possible judgement until his views can be evaluated on their scientific merit upon being aired in a public forum.

Dr. Thiessen's talk is an invited fellows address. I asked him to speak before our group and to provide me with a title for his presentation. He graciously accepted. I do not view my role as Program Chair to include censuring or editing titles of presentations (unless they exceed the 10-word limit specified by APA). Some titles will inevitably include words or innuendoes that offend someone or some group. Nor did I find Dr. Thiessen's title particularly offensive at the time of submission (though I now see how it could be interpreted in an offensive manner). Replacing the word "rape" with a more neutral synonym is not going to change the ugliness of the actual event which the terms represent. And, it is also the case that some forms of "rape" *are* pervasive in the animal kingdom (including homosexual rape among males—an event that heterosexual men find extremely repulsive when it occurs in our own species). If Dr. Thiessen's view is, as you suggest, that sexual violence against women (or men) is "acceptable or justifiable" due to our evolutionary heritage, it will be his responsibility as a scientist to adequately defend that view based on available evidence (or his interpretation of the evidence, which we are free to interpret differently and offer counter-arguments thereof). My own reaction to his title is not that rape is "acceptable or justifiable," but, rather, that it may be inevitable (and not necessarily adaptive) as a reproductive strategy, as has been shown in the case of mallard ducks by Hailman et al. — *Science*, 1978, 201:280–282).

These are very different positions, and I shall be shocked if Dr. Thiessen's view is the former; but, again, even if that's the case, it's his job as a scientist to defend whatever position he takes. As Program Chair, I am very eager to give him that opportunity rather than to, in any way, attempt to censure his viewpoints.

Again, I thank you for expressing your concern. I hope you will be able to attend Dr. Thiessen's session and argue your view against his publicly. After all, that's what science is all about.

Sincerely yours,

David B. Miller
Associate Professor
Program Chair of Division 6
 of APA
(Physiological & Comparative)

cc: Allan Mirsky
    Delbert Thiessen

APPENDIX C

The University of Connecticut
Storrs, Connecticut 06268

The College of
Liberal Arts and Sciences
Department of Psychology

August 4, 1983

Dr. David Miller
Campus U–20

Dear David,

By this time, you will have received a letter from Lila Braine with whom I talked recently about the title of Delbert Thiessen's invited Fellows' address at the upcoming APA meeting.

I, too, had noticed that his title stood out in the Division 6 program. It seemed offensive to me, somewhat along the lines of a title such as "Castrations: an effective method for increasing our enjoyment of opera." I don't know enough about Dr. Thiessen's field to know the jargon that is in everyday use but I should think that one would be very careful in a public lecture not to choose a title that could be perceived as tasteless, or that could be misconstrued by readers of the popular press.

It seems to me that over the years titles of all kinds of presentations, including Fellows' addresses, journal articles, and colloquia, have become cuter and cuter. Where will it all end? I could speculate on some reasons for this trend, not all of which are flattering to psychologists. However, my reason for writing to you as Program Chair of Division 6 is to ask that you raise the question of what might be done to discourage tasteless or sensational titles when you give your report to the Executive Committee. There must be some way to encourage the use of titles, perhaps through the Call for Papers, that would promote an awareness of APA's scientific virtues, rather than the image of Psychology that we are all too familiar with in the popular press.

Of course, it is difficult to legislate what people can or cannot do in their scientific presentations. Only journal editors have that privilege. But perhaps a climate could be created so that the possibility of confusing or offending could be minimized.

Sincerely,

Martha Wilson
Professor

cc. Allan Mirsky
    Delbert Thiessen

162

APPENDIX D

The University of Connecticut
Storrs, Connecticut 06268

The College of
  Liberal Arts and Sciences
Department of Psychology

August 4, 1983

Dr. Martha Wilson
Campus U–20

Dear Martha:

Thanks for your letter expressing concern about the title of Del Thiessen's Invited Fellows Address. I have already received Dr. Braine's letter and have responded to it. Rather than going through the same explanations twice, I am attaching a copy of my letter that I wrote to her.

Obviously, this is not an easy issue to resolve, as we are dealing with such issues as academic freedom and censorship on the one hand, and offensive language/ideologies on the other. I don't know Dr. Thiessen, so I don't know how he feels about this matter. But I am a little bit familiar with the "rape" literature in nonhuman organisms, and, as I told Dr. Braine, it is a fairly ubiquitous phenonemon in terms of the number of species in which it occurs, especially among waterfowl — the group with which I am most familiar. I no more believe that we are "doomed" (i.e., genetically determined) to become rapists than we are to do anything else; and, I feel the same is true among nonhumans. Rape occurs usually under certain environmental circumstances (e.g., overcrowding; preponderance of unmated males; etc.). The fact that it occurs in humans under certain circumstances (and I emphasize, *not* as a primary reproductive strategy that has been selected for through evolution!) hardly surprises me. This, in no way, renders rape justifiable. It is an ugly act, at least as viewed by most humans. (Humans tend to excel in ugly acts, which sets us apart from the majority of the animal kingdom.) I didn't mean to get off on this discourse, but these are some of the issues that could be addressed in a talk having the title that Dr. Thiessen chose. By the way, the comical title that you mentioned in your letter that could also be taken in an "offensive" manner, "Castration: An Effective Method for Increasing Our Enjoyment of Opera," is, as far as I can tell, rather inoffensive. If it were to be found that castration had such an effect, then each individual would have to weigh the pros and cons of fertility versus music appreciation. It's far-fetched, of course, but seemingly inoffensive (unless I am so insensitive an individual that I just can't perceive the issue).

Anyway, your suggestion about raising this issue at the Executive Committee meeting is useful, and I shall try to do at least that. As I said, this is no easy issue.

Sincerely,

David B. Miller
Associate Professor
Program Chair, Division 6

cc: Allan Mirsky
    Delbert Thiessen

163

APPENDIX E

Boston University Medical Center
85 East Newton Street
Boston, Massachusetts 02118
(617) 247-5479

Marlene Oscar Berman, Ph.D.
Director, Laboratory of Neuropsychology
Department of Biobehavioral Sciences

January 2, 1985

Ethel Tobach, Ph.D.
Curator, Comparative Psychology
American Museum of Natural History
Central Park West at 79th St.
New York, N.Y. 10024

Dear Ethel:

Regarding Thiessen:

I chaired the session in which he gave his fellow's address. There was a heated discussion after the talk, but Thiessen was unwilling to continue it in another room, despite the fact that a room had been arranged for such discourse. Most of the preconvention correspondence was conducted with David Miller at the University of Connecticut; he was the program chair. As Secretary, I received copies of the correspondence, I recall that Martha Wilson also wrote a good letter, as did Fran Graham. Perhaps you would like to contact them.

Later that year, Thiessen applied for membership in Division 35. Initially I was opposed to it, but I later withdrew my opposition in favor of Freedom of Expression. Let me know if you want to have more of my impressions.

Sincerely.

Marlene Oscar Berman, Ph.D.
Professor of Neurology
and Psychiatry

MOB/rr

AWP COMMENT ON THIESSEN'S TALK

The Association for Women in Psychology is an organization of women and men working for bias-free treatment of women and men in psychology. Since we saw the APA program listing Dr. Thiessen's talk, we have been distressed that the title exploits women, and uses the term and concept of rape in a sensationalizing way.

A number of psychologists have written concerned letters to the program Chair and to the President of Division 6. Because we feel that there are a number of serious issues involved in this case, we have requested the opportunity to make a formal comment.

Unfortunately Dr. Thiessen has not responded to our several attempts to discuss his paper before the conference, but in any case we feel it is less important to rebut specific points than it is to discuss three broader issues:

1) The sensational and exploitative nature of the title of this talk.
2) The downplay/ignoring of defining criteria for rape among humans, and
3) The question of academic freedom of speech.

First of all, the title of the talk is offensive to women and men because it implies that sexual violence by men against women is acceptable behavior, since it is our quote *legacy* unquote, and can be seen as quote *just a strategy* unquote.

Secondly, the title is distressing because it exploits rape and the condition of women who suffer rape, in a provocative, attention-getting way. Because the differences are great between human rape and the rare occurrence of forced copulation among animals, Thiessen's form of *sexual advertising* is clearly inappropriate in an academic forum like APA.

This brings us to the issue of criteria crucial to the understanding of human rape. While the lay-person's *myth* tends to focus on the *sexual* aspects of rape, serious scientists in the field know that two aspects are paramount in human rape: *violence*, and *lack of consent*. Forced copulation, the only component which certain animals might *seem* to share with humans IS NOT EVEN NECESSARY FOR A DEFINITION OF RAPE, NEITHER LEGALLY

IN CERTAIN STATES, NOR AMONG PSYCHOLOGISTS RE-SEARCHING THE ISSUE. *Violence* as humans practice it, and *lack of consent* are clearly issues which our science cannot start to evaluate in animal behavior. Thus generalizations from animal to human behavior are of dubious scholarly value.

Finally, we turn to the question of academic freedom. While we have serious doubts about the intellectual underpinnings of Thiessen's work on rape, we certainly support his right to report his ideas. What we find *in*supportable is the provocative and inflammatory, sensational way he chooses to publicize himself at the expense of women.

APPENDIX G

Division of Psychology of Women (Div. 35)
of the American Psychological Association

Irene Hanson Frieze, Ph.D.
Women's Studies Program
University of Pittsburgh
Pittsburgh, PA 15260
(412) 624-6485

October 3, 1983

Dr. Delbert D. Thiessen
Department of Psychology
University of Texas, Mezes Hall
Austin, TX 78712

Dear Dr. Thiessen,

The members of the Executive Committee of Division 35 (Psychology of Women) were quite concerned when we read the title of your talk on rape at APA. We find the implicit acceptance of the idea of rape as a reasonable means of having children quite upsetting. We wonder if you would have been equally willing to talk on "The Holocaust as a Population Control Strategy" or even "Lynching as Population Control"? An Equally degrading title might be "Castration as a Reproductive Strategy."

We assumed that your talk's title was casually chosen and that you had not thought carefully about the implications of your topic. We were surprised to hear you defend it after your talk.

I personally was also disappointed in your paper itself. In taking on this type of controversial issue, it would seem that you would have an extra responsibility, you relied mainly on correlational data to imply causality. For example, the high rape rates of young men were taken as a priori evidence that they rape to reproduce. No allowance was made for the generally higher crime rates of young men. There was also no evidence that poorly educated men have few children — you simply assumed this.

Perhaps the enclosed Guidelines for Nonsexist Research will provide you with more information about ways of avoiding sexism in the formulation of research questions and the interpretation of data.

Sincerely,

Irene Hanson Frieze, Ph.D.
President

mjh
cc: Aaron Canter, Ethel Tobach,
    Ellen Kimmel, Hannah Lerman,
    Mary Parlee, Charlene Depner
enclosure

APPENDIX H

The University of Texas at Austin
Austin, Texas 78712-7789

Department of Psychology
Mezes Hall 330

October 13, 1983

Dr. Irene Hanson Frieze
Women's Studies Program
University of Pittsburgh
Pittsburgh, PA 15260

Dear Dr. Frieze:

The mobilization of Division 35 women against my APA presentation was quite a shock and a clear demonstration of sexism on the part of an otherwise perceptive organization. I fear you misunderstand, both my motives and the dimensions of science. Perhaps I can clarify my points.

I certainly do not think that rape is a "reasonable means of having children." If you think I said that then I can understand why you are upset. Forcible rape is a serious crime and should be viewed as such. I am not defending the rapist, nor am I rationalizing the behavior. What I am seeking is an understanding as to why rape occurs — its environmental, physiological and phylogenetic correlates. My aim, in part, is similar to that of most women, namely to be able to reduce the incidence of rape. Therefore, I am particularly surprised that you oppose my efforts, rather than support them. Is my assumption correct that you do want to understand the facits [sic] of rape in order to do something constructive about it? Frankly, I am puzzled.

To reject outright the possibility of a biological interpretation of rape is a sad commentary on your perception of science. Should we not explore all possibilities in seeking answers to a critical social problem? Perhaps you believe that a biological approach assumes genetic determinism, and hence suggests that behaviors are unmodifiable. That is certainly not the case. All behaviors, particularly those of evolutionarily complex species, depend upon interactions between genes and environment. Rape, therefore, may have a phylogentic heritage, in that it apears to be associated with a polygynous mating style, but it is also facultative, changing dramatically with socioeconomic, sociological and psychological conditions.

What bothers me most about your reaction to my talk is the prescriptive nature of your attitude. It is conveying the impression that I should not investigate rape, and if I do I should begin with the assumptions you believe valid. You would even have me alter a title that directly speaks to my concerns because of what you read into it. To equate my title with the "Holocaust" or "Lynching" or any such derogatory association is both nonproductive and uninformed.

168

I have faith, however, that our basic motivations are in fact similar, even though our orientations differ. I would therefore like this letter to underline my belief that men and women should act together to further research that will uncover the hidden variables of rape and eventually lead to its irradication [sic]. With this as a premise I am therefore applying for membership in your worthwhile Division 35. Please accept this letter as my application for membership.

I look forward to hearing from you.

Sincerely,

Delbert D. Thiessen
Professor of Psychology

DDT/sm

c.c. Janet Spence
    Ethel Tobach
    Allen Mirsky

AUTHOR INDEX

SUBJECT INDEX

BIOGRAPHICAL SKETCHES

JULIE BLACKMAN, Ph.D. from Columbia Teacher's College, is an Assistant Professor of Psychology at Barnard College. Her research interests focus on physical and sexual abuse in families. She also has become involved with this in a courtroom setting by providing expert testimony.

FLORENCE DENMARK, Ph.D. from the University of Pennsylvania, is a Professor of Psychology at Hunter College and the Graduate School of the City University of New York. She has published extensively in the field of social psychology and the psychology of women. She has served as the President of the American Psychological Association (APA) in 1980, and is a former President of Psi Chi, of the Division of the Psychology of Women in APA (Division 35), and of the New York State Psychological Association. She is currently President-Elect of the Eastern Psychological Association. She has been honored as a Mellon Scholar at St. Olaf College and with an Outstanding Woman in Science Award by the Association for Women in Science.

SUSAN FRIEDMAN is working towards her B.A. at the City University of New York, where she is majoring in psychology and women's studies. She has been a professional actress for ten years and is currently appearing in the hit musical, "KuniLeml" in New York. She is also working on a book about the Jewish actress in America.

CHERYL HARDING, Ph.D. from the Institute of Animal Behavior — Rutgers University, is an Associate Professor of Psychology at Hunter College and the Graduate School of the City University of New York. She is also a Research Associate in the Departments of Animal Behavior and Ornithology at the American Museum of Natural History, and an Adjunct Associate Professor of Behavioral Sciences at Rockefeller University. Her research is on the relationship between hormones and sexual, aggressive, and social behavior in avian species.

Sarah Lenington, Ph.D. in Biology from the University of Chicago, is an Assistant Professor at the Institute of Animal Behavior — Rutgers University. Previously, she held a postdoctoral fellowship in Epidemiology, where her work focused on child abuse. Her current research concerns behavior genetics of wild house mice.

Herman Schwendinger, Ph.D. in Sociology from the University of California, Los Angeles, is a Professor of Sociology at the State University of New York at New Paltz.

Julia Siegel Schwendinger, Ph.D. in Criminology from the University of California, Berkeley, is an Adjunct Assistant Professor of Sociology at the State University of New York at New Paltz. She has served as a Deputy Parole Commissioner in the San Francisco Sheriff's Department and as the Director of the Women's Resource Program. She was a founder of Bay Area Women Against Rape in Berkeley, the first rape crisis center in the world.

The Schwendingers have published widely in journals of criminology and sociology and have written several books. They were founders of the journal, *Crime and Social Justice*, and were the 1984 Tappan Award winners for outstanding contributions to criminology.

Suzanne Sunday, Ph.D. in BioPsychology from Rutgers University, is an Assistant Professor of Psychology at Manhattanville College. She is also the Coordinator of the Women's Studies Program. Her research focuses on feeding behavior in a variety of rodent species.

Ethel Tobach, Ph.D. in Psychology from New York University, is a comparative psychologist at the American Museum of Natural History. She is also an Adjunct Professor in the Psychology Department at Hunter College, and in the Biology Department at the City College of New York. Her research is on the evolution and development of social-emotional behavior. She has written extensively on the role of science in societal processes leading to racism and sexism.

DATE DUE